How To Invest
If You Can't
Afford To Lose

TOM GLEASON

ISBN: 1463750307
ISBN-13: 9781463750305

Library of Congress Control Number: 2011916560
CreateSpace, North Charleston, SC

NOTE TO READERS

How to Invest If You Can't Afford to Lose contains the opinions and ideas of the author. The author is not a lawyer or a tax expert. The strategies outlined in this book will not suit every individual. No warranties or guarantees exist with regard to the realization of a satisfactory result. If legal advice or other expert assistance is required, seek the services of a competent professional.

Contents

INTRODUCTION

Economic systems in America and Europe are struggling with debt and unfavorable demographic trends. Emerging markets have become the beneficiaries of jobs and capital flows. It's a new world and ten years of market crashes is proof investors can't be complacent and hope for the best. They need to take action now to reduce risk and grow their assets. Investors can achieve better results by avoiding the high fees and self-serving advice offered by Wall Street. Market timing techniques I've developed can beat the buy and hold returns of major stock indexes across the world. How to Invest If You Can't Afford to Lose is about higher returns and reduced risk.

Part One of the book talks about the individual investor and the investment products that are available to them. I start with investor psychology and show why it too often leads to failure. Fear causes people to seek solutions from brokers and bankers and their products always come with diminished performance and high fees. Several heavily marketed and terrible investment ideas are explained. Then asset classes are presented with charts showing the historical returns. The reader learns how to combine them to achieve returns that can consistently beat the best pension funds. The whole investment process is explained in a way the average person will find easy to grasp. At the end of Part One, the reader will be convinced and confident they can win at investing.

Part Two is for investors who'd like to get superior returns by using market timing. I show how the average person can beat the major stock indexes from New York to Bombay with much less risk. The investor can buy in near low points and sell near the high points. The techniques are simple and only require checking prices once a month. Explore market indexes around the world for opportunity. I show how to time the S&P500, NASDAQ, Gold,

Bonds, Commodities plus markets in China, England, Germany, Japan, Brazil and India. I discuss gold as a hedge against disaster. We wind down with discussions on real estate and some investment philosophy.

The way to financial independence certainly requires saving some money. More important, is getting a good rate of return. Most important, is having confidence in a plan proven to work over many years. If you can gain knowledge and confidence, then you won't sabotage your efforts by panicking in and out of the market.

If you can't afford to lose, then risk is everything. Winning at investing can be done and I'll prove it to you. I'll show you simple and innovative ways to self-manage your investment money with a conservative asset mix. I'll show you how to time your entry and exit points into the financial markets to avoid steep losses. If you can read, you can win. You have everything it takes to be successful.

In this book, I'll explain methods that grow wealth and provide a life of security. There is no such thing as certainty in this life. However, I am confident that you will succeed at safely growing your savings, if you follow a few simple steps. The results will exceed what you thought was possible. If you've been fearful about investing, then this is the book you've been waiting for.

PART ONE

"the poor man seeks riches
the rich man seeks heaven
the wise man seeks equilibrium"

- Anonymous

1

WHO SHOULD READ THIS BOOK

This book is for people anywhere in the world who need to invest but are concerned about losing their money. Because of age or temperament, losing is not an outcome they can accept. You have every right to be concerned. With volatile markets, bad advice, high fees and just general confusion about what to do, many people simply do nothing or hand over their savings to a stranger to manage. Fear prevents many people from investing and succeeding at necessary goals. Large previous losses may have left a deep psychological scar.

It's true. Investors across the world face an uncertain future, with governments in debt and trust placed in leaders frequently betrayed. A sure sign of distress is when currencies fall against gold. Tyranny is certain when citizens are not allowed to own gold. The answer for investors is not speculation, blind faith or placing all your money into a narrow asset class.

Financial markets can protect investor wealth, if money is properly allocated among asset classes. Much higher returns with greater safety are possible if the investments are sold before steep declines in the market. It's my belief that millions of investors need a way to get better returns. They want protection from bad advice and excessive risk. They want their money to grow every year and preferably with a rate of return better than a pension fund. They want protection from inflation and recessions. If those ideas sound appealing, then this book is for you.

Fear of losing money is widespread. Large losses are usually devastating and can't be recovered by hard work. Fear isn't irrational and must not be ignored. Large investment losses are caused by both severe market declines and over-concentration of money in a single asset class. When a portfolio is properly balanced with the right assets and in equilibrium with the investor's psychological makeup then good things can happen. When it's out of balance, the investor moves money around out of fear, does nothing or relies on others for advice. The end result is often financial failure.

Investors face a difficult time getting good financial advice. Employers won't provide advice for fear of being sued. Investment advisors you pick from the phone book or from brokerage firms all want a percentage of your assets and they never protect you against large market declines. They all tend to make money management sound complicated. Much advice comes with a serious conflict of interest. Many investors conclude that doing well is impossible.

Here's the truth. Successful investing is easy. The Financial Services Industry (aka Wall Street in America) makes it sound complicated because they exist to collect fees off your money. If you're stressed about investing, then you need to break ranks with Wall Street. In this book I offer portfolios that avoid over concentration in a single asset class. This alone will greatly reduce losses in a market crash and puts you far ahead of the average investor. But that's not enough. You need to do well in both recessions and booms. I'm going to show you how to win with ideas that will stand the test of time. I'm confident your capital will be protected and any objective financial expert reviewing your performance will say, "How did you figure this out? Good job!"

In 2011 the first baby boomers reached 65 years old. They've just gone through ten years of horrific market turmoil that has pummeled their assets. A younger generation finds itself in competition with emerging economies. America never had a strong social contract between workers and employers. But now, even the implicit agreement with the government providing promised retirement benefits is failing. Young and old can't afford to lose. A smarter way to invest and grow capital is needed.

EXAMPLES OF PEOPLE WHO CAN'T AFFORD TO LOSE

A retired couple living on fixed income from their savings can't afford to lose their capital because one or both might then have to go back to work. Health problems or just a need to relax after many years of work makes that thought unacceptable. Like most people in this position, they invest their savings in super safe government bonds and reap meager returns. They're troubled because their yearly asset drawdown makes it likely they'll outlive their savings. They may end up dependent on family members. For this investing couple, safety is first but better returns are needed.

A woman aged 50, saving for retirement, trusted her advisor and lost badly in the latest stock market crash. This was a fearful experience and now she sits mostly in cash and bonds but knows the returns on those assets won't achieve her goal of retiring at 62. She needs to see her money grow and never go backwards. Psychologically, she can't accept another financial setback. She wonders if she can grow her capital without taking losses.

A young man in mid career is struggling to save but finds his yearly returns never seem to match the S&P500 index. His financial advisor is charging a 1% yearly fee and he doesn't understand what the advisor is doing or why. A little research shows that his mutual fund expense fees are very high compared to an index fund. He knows the costs are too much and wonders if he can do better. He's too busy to become an expert on investing and would like a simple way to invest that he can understand.

A couple is helping their elderly parents manage their money. They must preserve the assets so the folks have money to live on, but the brothers and sisters are worried they may not do a good job. The family is concerned about losing their inheritance. They ask about hiring a money manager. The advisor proposes a 1% yearly commission or says to buy an annuity through him. He offers no assurance that he can avoid the next 40% market crash. The couple wonders if there's a better way to appease the family and safely provide an adequate living income for the parents.

An investor is concerned about the economy collapsing due to government debt and other perceived economic ills. She believes gold or real estate could be a core asset but is hesitant. How can she come out ahead in a world turned upside down.

The Five Types of Investors

The majority of people who invest money for future objectives can be classified five ways. These groupings are based on their emotional temperament and investing style. I believe asset choices are driven by a person's placement along an emotional continuum that ranges between fear and over-confidence.

Group 1. This group invests in various assets but primarily they use a jumble of mutual funds. They have a poor grasp of investment finance and make decisions based on media recommendations, advice from friends or they follow popular trends. They lack confidence in their actions but keenly feel the need to succeed. They tend to panic and sell when the market has a correction and buy back later at higher prices. Their long term results are usually poor. If they use an advisor he gets frequent calls.

Group 2. This group prefers not to deal with investment details and will stay with whatever plan is offered by their employer or advisor. They don't understand financial markets very well, but fear is usually offset by complacency. Often an investment advisor is used and they pay the asking rate and give little attention to fees and fund expenses. Long-term results can be quite good if they're well advised, but the opposite can also occur. There's a high likelihood of underperformance due to costs, but it's not noticed. This group is at risk during deep market declines.

Group 3. Investors here may have advanced after years of failure or a realization that complacency has been costly. They invest in index funds to a great extent and pay a lot of attention to costs and performance. They understand the need for portfolio balance and are unlikely to use a commission advisor but may pay a fixed fee for yearly advice. Market knowledge may be only average. Risk is managed with asset allocation. Fear is present, but is checked by rationality and emotional control. Long-term results are good.

Group 4. Market knowledge may be exceptional and the tendency is towards over-confidence. They analyze, investigate, discuss stocks and markets and exhibit a fascination with trading and guessing market trends. They pay for investment research, follow the news and various technical indicators and trade frequently. Results are often poor.

Group 5. This class of investor is rare. They use the asset allocation methods of Group 3 but also use simple market timing methods to avoid steep declines in asset classes. They beat investment advisors, the S&P500 index and the best pension funds. Their returns are in the upper 10% of all investors.

My research shows fear is a major factor not just in financial markets, but in investment style. Groups 1 and 4 exhibit poor emotional control but they're at different extremes. Group 1 is edgy and can't stay with anything and group 4 is always trying to hit a home run. Groups 2 and 3 have less fear and less confidence and tend to be more successful.

Group 2 investors are complacent but tend to stay with a program. Group 3 outperforms the others by managing fear and using balance to design their investment plan. They'll take advice if they understand it. Group 5 greatly outperforms because they sell before market crashes and then buy back much lower. Performance can be stunning.

This book is designed primarily for the conservative investor who needs to win. The simple market timing strategies can also be used by the aggressive investor in a concentrated portfolio.

2

EMBRACE FEAR

Fear is a powerful emotion and is necessary for survival. It's instinctive. Human behavior is grounded in ancient, hard-wired survival patterns. We survived while living in a tribe because we watched for predators. We often dismiss fear today and talk of "fearless leaders" in the areas of politics and business. In the old days, being fearless got you killed and your gene line terminated. Fear is not an enemy or something to be ashamed of; it's a means of sustaining life. It speaks with a roar when a sudden danger approaches. The entire body goes on high alert as adrenaline surges and the senses become acute. Fear speaks with a quiet voice when your intuition suggests something isn't quite right. Embrace fear as a true friend and think of it as the inner warrior, always on guard and ready to defend you.

THE FOUR FOUNTAINS

The ancients described the four fountains of life as food, sleep, sex, and self preservation. They spoke of the importance of managing the fountains carefully. Proper regulation of these forces creates balance. When the intellect properly manages the flow of the fountains, it's called self control. Good judgment must always be in charge or the mind is thrown into confusion.

We live in unbalanced times. Food is required for life but people are fat from too much of it. Sex is required to maintain the species but if misdirected it ruins relationships. Sleep is essential, but when neglected due to stress, it causes the mind to make mistakes. Self preservation in the form of FEAR steps forward to defend you when the intellect senses danger or sees something it doesn't understand. Fear is needed for emergency actions. Persistent fear indicates that that the intellect is not in control of a situation and doesn't understand how to solve a problem.

Modern corporate marketers know all about fear. They hire psychologists to help them with their advertising so fear is not awakened. That's why on TV you see handsome, smiling people offering loans. We aren't defensive against strangers who smile at us. Advertisements show absolutely joyous people gambling in casinos when common sense tells you these people are fools, throwing away their money. Still, the casino business thrives, even in bad times. Marketers have learned to reduce fear by marketing debt and foolishness as fun. The best defense is good judgment. There's little of that in Las Vegas or on Wall Street.

Sometimes marketers try to induce fear, if they want to sell a financial service. They create a problem and then show how their product fixes it. Life insurance and annuities are about fear and are sold at high profit by Wall Street to consumers.

Governments and unscrupulous politicians use fear all the time to gain support for their actions. They create a straw man, a non-existent enemy, to induce fear and repeat the danger story until people accept it. They plant news articles that put another country or a suggested reform in a bad light. They hope to create worry and unease and then propose a costly or oppressive solution.

My favorite example of fear mongering was after 9/11 when the US government told people to build huts of plastic sheets in the living room to protect against anthrax. This was idiotic but it worked – certainly never against anthrax, but against reason. They created a climate of fear as a prelude to war. If the public buys into the fear, they'll soon ask for a solution.

It doesn't stop there. Governments use catch phrases like "The War on Drugs" to evoke images of doing battle against people with syringes. "No Child Left Behind" evokes an image of a little kid all alone as mom and dad drive away. "Global Warming" has the tide carrying grandma's poodle out to sea. Media experts also create campaigns for large corporations and politicians who hope to profit from government policy dollars. Sometimes the policy is good and the ad campaigns may actually be useful, but the experts know the public at large responds more strongly to emotion than reason. Fear is a great motivator.

Nature never intended for your friend, FEAR, to be on high alert all the time. Fear consumes a lot of energy. Unresolved fear is called stress and it's epidemic in modern societies. Doctors know it wreaks havoc with health. People worry about their job, paying the bills and even worry about looking good to the opposite sex. Stress is definitely not helpful for investing.

People are stressed about investing because they're afraid to lose money and that's a valid self preservation issue. Fear about money won't go away unless people see a solution to the problem, even if it's a mirage. Wall Street offers a high priced solution so the consumer can relax – that is until the market crashes and they discover the "solution" didn't protect their savings.

People with little fear are called gullible or over-confident. They often lose their life savings believing a lie. If there's too much fear about money, a person won't invest and refuses to take reasonable risks. So, how can fear be regulated to reduce the stress about investing? Most people turn their money over to a financial advisor who steers them into high fee mutual funds. The funds and the advisor each take 1% off the top but the customer's fear goes away because they're hopeful someone is looking out for them. This is a failure behavior but a logical response to a persistent stress situation. Don't feel ashamed if this has been your response to fears about investing.

Fear must be regulated by knowledge. If you have a weapon certain to defeat your enemy, then you aren't fearful and can act with confidence. When your intellect understands the problem and sees a solution that makes sense then Fear can withdraw; confidence is then regained and the body relaxes. When FEAR knows your investments are safe he steps back but continues to watch with calm alertness.

In this book, I'll show you how to invest and how to win in the short and long term. You'll learn how to get better returns with less risk. By managing risk, we acknowledge fear, but balance it with reason. It's the correct way to regulate and achieve balance in life. It's also the key to enjoying the good long term returns offered by the financial markets. You'll gain confidence and your investments will grow.

3

THE WALL STREET CONFIDENCE GAME

A Confidence Game is a swindle in which the victim is defrauded after confidence has been won. One of the most effective forms of this scam is called "Affinity Fraud". It means being cheated by someone you know and have no reason to mistrust. Fraud works best in a climate of perceived safety. Longtime employees are trusted by their employer and can exploit a situation in ways a new employee never could. I worked as a fraud auditor for several years and saw it firsthand.

Criminals often offer to do favors and this serves to obtain a higher level of access to inside information. The victim is made to feel like someone cares about them enough to help out. This fake concern is effective, especially with the elderly. Studies have shown that, as people age, they tend to think better of general society and become more trusting. They're susceptible to being cheated by family members and by salesmen. It's sad to witness the effects this has on decent and ethical old people.

My uncle Art worked in the parts department of a major car manufacturer for thirty years. When he was older he was often cheated because he trusted everyone. We went to his house one day and saw he had purchased new windows and doors for the home. On closer inspection I saw that the storm windows were all ill fitting. The doors had 2" gaps at the bottom. Gypsy con artists going door-to-door had scammed poor uncle Artie. This little story is funny in hindsight, but it's an example of what happens when people lack good judgment or self control. If ignorance is present and Fear is subdued, the criminal's job becomes easy.

On a humorous note, Artie also bought cancer insurance policies from any salesman who called. He eventually died of lung cancer (he smoked two packs a day). When my father opened his safe deposit box, he found cancer insurance policies worth over $125,000 with my impoverished aunt as the beneficiary. This was in 1985 dollars! What a windfall for my aunt who had been abandoned in poor health by her husband for another woman. She now had a second chance at life!

I recently read a news story about members of a church who were conned into buying Iraqi Dinars – a near worthless currency. The fraudster enlisted the services of a naïve church member and paid him commissions. The congregation had an affinity with this person and invested. The scam netted million of dollars and many church members lost their life savings. This points out an important fact. Developing a position of trust is an effective cover for people intent on profiting from fraud.

I have a friend, a retired rocket scientist, who worked on NASA projects. Needless to say he's a smart guy. He told me of his fears about losing money in the markets and how he checked his portfolio every day. If the market had a modest correction of a few percent, he got on the phone to his financial advisor and told him to do something so he wouldn't lose any more money. This sounds ridiculous, and it is, but his fear is real.

He had no idea that mutual funds charged fees to cover their costs and provide a profit. He thought the 1% charged by his advisor was his only expense. Clearly, he wasn't told the facts or chose not to ask. I told him how the various fees worked and suggested he manage his own money to cut costs. He abruptly held his hands to his ears and shook his head rapidly back and forth and asked me to stop talking. He said he worries about the market all the time and just can't handle thinking about it or making any decisions by himself. He didn't want to know. Like I said, bad money management has little to do with intelligence. Some people just have no desire to master the little basics required to be successful and would rather be tiger bait.

There's an old adage: "Neither a borrower nor a lender be". This is good advice and nowadays is universally ignored by the majority of people. People borrow against their homes to finance current consumption. They're not fearful because they believe they'll earn enough in the future to pay off the debts. Self-delusion is just another form of affinity fraud – everyone does it so it must be ok. Wall Street is always right there to help.

There's another old adage: "Never loan money to a relative and expect to get it back." My experience shows that saying to be quite true. Yet people keep "loaning" money to their adult kids and go to their grave without seeing a nickel of it. This happens because people trust their family members. That's generally good and natural but even generous people need to be realistic when it comes to money.

As you can tell, I like wise old sayings. They're generally true. However, with all this good advice floating down through the millennia, why do people keep making the same mistakes? They didn't always. Only during the boom years after 1950 did people become so complacent. The WWII generation is passing on, along with its memories of the bad old days. The lessons were forgotten as fear was subdued.

Fear has come back with difficult economic conditions. Homes are falling in value and incomes are stagnant as employment opportunities fall away. People withdraw their money from investments in order to cover their bills. They expect Armageddon, but to their amazement, some financial markets do well despite poor general economic conditions. How can that be? They think, if only they had invested earlier they could recover their losses. So, they buy again at the top and lose again.

I believe it's important to be on guard when it comes to money. That doesn't mean you should do nothing or put all your cash in a bank savings account. Successful investing requires listening to Fear and his many concerns. Give him the knowledge he needs. He'll appreciate it and can then relax for a while. Fear and Knowledge are both necessary for success.

Don't Be Complacent

The world economic systems are coalescing in a pattern popularly called "globalization". Some effects are the expansion of global corporate operations, a reduction in the number of currencies and more free trade between nations. Corporations need to keep costs competitive across regions. One way to accomplish that goal is to eliminate guaranteed pension plans and push the management of retirement assets onto the workers. At the same time, governments want to reduce social service commitments including retirement benefits and health care. Workers are losing guaranteed benefits while wages stagnate due to global competitive pressures. This doesn't bode well for financial security in old age.

Retirement risks are increasing for workers. For most workers these changes will not have a good outcome due to widespread ignorance about how to save, where to invest, who to trust, when to buy and sell and so forth. This ubiquitous problem means people will turn more to financial services companies and financial planners for help. This help will come at a high cost and with no protection from market crashes. People who take this path are certain to get lower returns than they should.

Employers are allowed to offer some advice to employees about investment options. The reality is this advice will either come from a person in the human resources department or, more likely, from a commission financial consultant brought in as a general purpose advisor. Employees will be steered to the most expensive option offered by the advisor. You don't want to take that path. It's unnecessary, costly and will delay achieving your financial objectives. Here's a little secret. The average financial planner has all the problems and stresses of everyone else you know. Look around – there are a lot of educated people with serious emotional and financial problems.

Advisors need to make a living off of other people's money. As representatives of insurance companies and Wall Street firms, they're trained to sell financial products that generate high fees. In the absence of good information and honest advice, many people will choose the high cost plans that sap the returns available for their assets. They'll follow the status quo and down they go. Others, with better information, will choose to maximize their saving dollars and take advantage of the smarter options offered by retirement plans.

Without a doubt, if you're reading this book you've got some smarts and have some initiative. Otherwise, the title wouldn't have resonated with you. You also have the instincts to wonder how lower costs and better performance could make a huge difference in the future. In the pages ahead you'll see what the effect of costs and mismanagement really means to you. You'll be shown choices that work and you won't need to hire someone for expensive advice – unless you choose to.

After I explain the investing basics, I'll show you how to create a balanced portfolio. Next, I'll show you how to time the markets to obtain investment returns that exceed the best pension funds. A market timing calculation can be done once a month on the back of an envelope.

The average financial planner is usually a decent and honest person and I'm not suggesting otherwise or that excessive abuse exists. However, they gear their products toward the average, uninformed person and invariably find ways to charge high fees. You truly don't need them. Investors must always be on guard against the enormous financial services industry. It is habituated to skimming off worker wealth and taking every opportunity to increase its profits.

Financial regulations have turned decidedly against the consumer. Wall Street contributes money to political campaigns and gets to write the legislation. The politicians and Wall Street are in cahoots. It's so crooked it's laughable.

As a society, we've brought this abuse and rapacious greed upon ourselves. People buy cars more expensive than they can afford. Buying on credit to obtain the latest fad is commonplace and especially with the young. Saving is out of style. Wall Street doesn't need to hard sell people on stupid ideas. They just offer up platters of bad choices to a willing public.

The Enemy is Clever

Wall Street marketers know all about fear and trust. That's why they have logos showing the Rock of Gibraltar, use celebrity spokesmen, name their firms after historical patriots and use words symbolizing trust and fidelity. They also have pretty brochures with smiling families on the cover and a well dressed representative who oozes concern.

The large financial services companies operate a confidence game. They sell their services to small investors as a form of protection; basically as a defense against doing something dumb. People figure these firms have some extra special skill that prevents them from losing lots of money. There's one problem with this picture of confidence and success. The big firms consistently underperform the market averages and consistently charge customers huge fees. The customer is robbed a little every year rather than in one big grab. It's a legal form of fraud. Wall Street is a tiger in pinstripes. The key to deluding the masses is to create a climate of trust.

You may think that I'm too harsh on financial advisors and your guy is different or your situation is more complicated. You placed your trust in someone because he is so honest and caring. I'll tell you this. Always have your guard up when dealing with money issues. A healthy skepticism hurts no one and can save your financial life.

Don't Lose to Globalization

Look around at the enormous shifts of jobs to Asia, the dismantling of employer pension plans and huge increases in health care costs. Soon, we'll witness the tear down of government old age support and new constraints placed on Social Security. These are not signals of expanding worker prosperity for Americans. The traditional corporation is becoming a global entity and they are shedding the support systems they provided to workers for three generations.

These changes appear negative to people in the West because we have to compete with the lower cost structures of developing nations. Conversely, the mega-trend into globalization means positive changes and great opportunity to people in other parts of the world. Globalization is positive and profitable for public companies overall.

It's clear; workers will be responsible for managing their own financial futures and not employers or the government. Wall Street is already profiting immensely from globalization and the instant-information of the Internet. Globalization is creating the strange situation in America where workers are at risk but investors could see returns in the years ahead that perhaps equal the best decades of the 20th century. That isn't a prediction. Voter discontent with income inequality could produce a political backlash that curtails globalization.

Since we're likely to see continued constraints on worker income growth, it's essential that people get the best possible returns on their invested money. You can profit in the financial markets if you do just a few things right and avoid a few major mistakes. Turn the tables on Wall Street. It's never been easier to do. The result will be less risk and higher returns.

ACT NOW TO PROTECT YOUR WEALTH

In America investors face a long term, declining dollar amid a massive buildup of public debt. The expanding level of government debt and reckless spending cannot be sustained. What should an investor do? Holding cash and bonds loses to inflation. Stocks could lose big during a deep recession. Wall Street's dead-wrong and expensive advice didn't help investors during the last crash and it probably won't help against recession, a depression or future inflation. It's essential to open your eyes and invest in the right mixes of assets that can survive and prosper under uncertain market conditions. Low costs and properly balancing risk and performance are the right way to invest. In addition, you need the right mix of assets invested at the right time. You can do it and without Wall Street picking your pocket.

4

Costs, Performance and Risk

With investments everyone would like low costs, high return performance and low risk. For many people 'reasonable risk' means they never want to lose money. Sure, getting good returns would be nice but not losing is more important for preserving capital. I think not losing is a reasonable request but that shouldn't mean accepting low returns. Fear of loss is the reason why people invest in certificates of deposit and why they buy annuities.

Psychological research has revealed that the fear response of losing a certain sum of money exceeds the pleasure response of winning the same amount of money by 2:1. This means that fears of investment loss are common and are a powerful motivator to avoid taking on risk. The fear response is a hard-wired defense mechanism and is stronger in some people than others. It's <u>not</u> foolish to feel fearful about losing money.

Reducing potential losses is critical for many people. This fear of loss is brushed off by the popular media, which likes to glamorize people who take on huge risks and win. You often see mutual fund ads showing the average return over a time period. Do you ever see ads showing how they never had a loss in 10 or 20 years? Never! That's because they want investors to focus on winning, so they avoid the fear issue of losing. Yet every investor knows that mutual funds lose and, sometimes, in a very big way. People fail at investing because they feel it's too dangerous, so they accept low risk and low returns. Some turn their financial affairs over to brokers, or relatives or play the lottery.

Here's a fact. A passive portfolio can be designed that rarely loses and the loss will modest. The components of a good portfolio have to work together to achieve the right balance. When properly balanced, the portfolio will provide appealing returns. Add a little market timing and it becomes a powerhouse. Wait till you see how easy it is to do. This more active approach reduces losses during down markets and offers big opportunities to buy early into rising markets. This combination can dramatically improve your yearly returns. It can be done with low cost index funds available to everyone and a simple market timing technique.

What's an index fund? It's a mutual fund that contains all the stocks in a certain segment of the market. There's an index for big companies, small companies, medium sized companies, real estate, commodities, international stocks and other asset classes. There is no stock picking involved in building an index. When you buy an index fund you get every company that meets the index criteria.

The Dow Jones Industrial Average is the most famous index and holds thirty stocks. It's discussed all the time on the news. The S&P500 is the most commonly tracked index and consists of the 500 largest US firms. The financial industry compares the performance of mutual funds to the S&P500. Doing better than this index for even a few years is a very big deal among money managers.

Index funds are cost efficient because there's little trading involved and the management costs are minimal. The expense fee of Vanguard's S&P500 index fund is .17 percent. Managed funds are 1.14 percent. Yet, an S&P500 index fund outperforms the managed mutual funds. The same performance advantage holds true for other indexes too like those that track small company stocks. It's hard to consistently beat the performance of an index fund.

In the pages ahead I'll show you how to combine index funds to reap diversification of assets, good performance and rock bottom costs. You won't have to learn much beyond what I've already discussed. Now, please understand this next point.

Index funds have average market risk. Owning an index fund does not mean the fund won't lose money. However, the right mix

of index funds in a portfolio creates an almost magical balance of performance. This balance protects your wealth against deep losses. One purpose of this book is to show you how to create balance.

COSTS

If you invest in mutual funds, your investment costs include fees charged by the fund plus any fees you pay to an advisor. The typical stock mutual fund charges over 1% in management fees on every dollar invested. Regardless of how the fund performs, you have to pay this every year. Many investors have a financial advisor and they typically charge at least 1% of your assets every year. Again, this comes right off the top.

So, if the broad stock market rises by 8% one year, then the mutual fund and the advisor likely take a combined 2%. That leaves you with 6%. You take all the risk and they get 25% of your returns. Does that sound fair? No! It's ridiculous! This is the price you pay for being a victim of the Wall Street confidence game. The actual effect of fees is really much worse.

The next chart shows what happens to a $10,000 initial investment over twenty years when 1.75% in expenses and advisor fees are taken every year, versus only the .18% charged by an index fund. The high fee fund grows to $36,900, but the index fund grows to $49,400. Over 20 years, the fees steal $12,500 of the gains. You could have had 46% more profit (12,500/26,900).

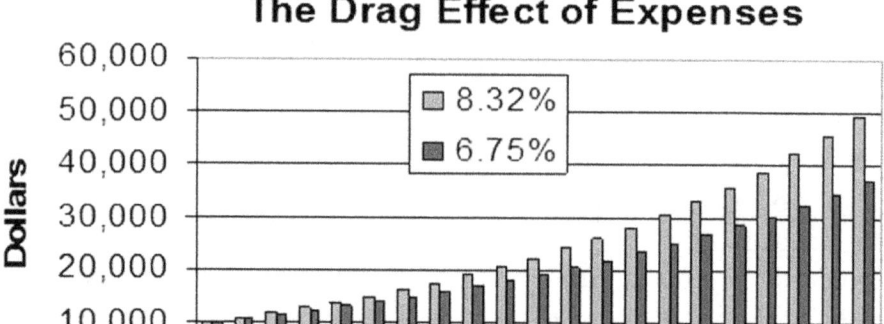

It gets even worse. Some advisors move your money to high expense mutual fund companies that charge additional 'load fees" at the time of purchase. The 5% Load Fee (Sales Charge) on the initial purchase of many mutual funds is split between the fund and your friendly advisor. The advisor should be looking out for you. Instead, they take 1% of your money each year whether you win or lose and then set you up for another pummeling. If the fund performance is bad and you move the money to another fund with the same company, you can be charged the fee again. If you pay a 5% front-end load fee, your money only grows to $35,000. Fees have now taken 30% of the potential gain.

Some funds charge a "back end load" (a deferred sales charge) rather than front end loads. This is common on funds offered through insurance companies. These insidious charges can run well over 5%, thus locking you into a spiraling hellhole of fees and expenses.

These fee levels are not unusual; it's typical. It gets worse. Even after subtracting fees, the average managed mutual fund under-performs an index fund by another 1% due to frequent trading and tax inefficiency. Your total costs could easily equal 3% per year by using an advisor and managed mutual funds.

Don't pay anyone a 3% yearly tax on your own money! Average costs of your mutual fund portfolio should be no more than .25% and that's why you need to use index funds. With an index fund portfolio, you don't need a commission financial advisor. This means your money can grow at least an extra 2.5% every year and with less risk.

PERFORMANCE

As a class, managed mutual funds consistently underperform index funds that invest in the same market segment. This is primarily due to expenses. Some funds may outperform for a few years, but then slip back. You can't predict who will outperform next year or over any other time period. Numerous studies show that costs hold back the performance of managed funds.

Mutual funds are compared against a benchmark. Funds that buy large company stocks are benchmarked against the S&P500 index. A fund investing in small company stocks is benchmarked against an index of "small cap stocks". It's important to compare a fund's performance against the appropriate benchmark.

Some funds have skilled managers who do well against the index for an extended period. That's rare and these guys are the cream of the crop - for a while. It's a lot like a team having a superstar ball player. Alas, even the best players fade with time and revert to average or lower. Their investing theme suddenly no longer works. This usually happens after a period of good performance has boosted cash inflows into the fund. It becomes harder to manage huge sums.

Index funds provide the average return of the entire market segment they represent. Poor performers are gradually dropped from the index and the winners move up. It's automatic. Thus, it's impossible for an index fund to underperform the average.

RISK

Risk includes the volatility of the mutual fund. "Volatility" is the normal up and down movement each year for a mutual fund. Often, this depends on the asset class it's in. A technology fund, whose share price often goes wildly up and down, is called volatile.

A fund invested solely in gold, technology, mining shares, health care or any narrow market segment is risky because it's susceptible to big drops in price. The same holds for individual stocks. If earnings fall because of a competitor comes out with a popular product, the share price can plummet.

Here's a point to understand about managed mutual funds. A high one-time mutual fund return is often the result of the fund manager taking on more risk. In other words, he makes a big bet that a certain sector, like pharmaceuticals, takes off and provides outsized returns. This "theme investing" can work in reverse when ideas flop. As an investor in a managed fund, you don't really know what the fund manager is up to. With an index fund, you know exactly what the fund owns and can be certain the fund's risk never exceeds that of the market.

THE FALSE PROTECTION OF CONSERVATIVE MUTUAL FUNDS

Risk is increased whenever assets are over-concentrated. Many cautious investors hold risky portfolios and it's hard to convince them otherwise. Let me explain a common situation.

Every mutual fund family offers one or more funds that hold a conservative mix of stocks plus some bonds. These go by various names like Equity-Income, Balanced, Asset Allocation, Retirement Growth and Life-Cycle. They differ based on the percentage of stocks owned versus bonds. The stock percent can range from 40-70%. I have no problem with these balanced-type funds on one condition. They should be seen for what they are - a mix of bonds and large company stocks.

A 60ish retired woman recently asked me how she should invest her money. She was being terribly over-charged by a bank invest-ment advisor who placed her cash into mutual funds with huge expenses. I suggested one of the portfolios in this book, but told her that I don't manage money for people and never act as a paid advisor. I urged her to first consult with her long-time CPA to get a second opinion. She did. He liked my idea of using index funds but had "a few other suggestions". Instead of index funds, he told her to place her money into "conservative" funds. Here was his portfolio.

Vanguard Wellington Fund (VWELX)
Vanguard Asset Allocation Fund (VAAPX)
Vanguard Balanced Fund (VBINX)

All mutual funds are listed on the exchanges by five letter names. The X at the end means mutual fund. Loading up a portfo-lio with several balanced funds is bad financial management, but is a widespread practice among financial advisors. Many believe that if a balanced-type fund is good, then more of them are even better.

VWELX, VAAPX, and VBINX are all essentially the same mutual fund with varying percentages of bonds. If you look at what they hold, they differ little from countless others with the same investment objective. They all hold big company, dividend paying stocks and some bonds. Look at the top 5 holdings of each fund.

Vanguard Wellington Fund
Exxon, ATT, Chevron, Wells Fargo, Pfizer
Vanguard Asset Allocation Fund
Exxon, Apple, Chevron, GE, IBM
Vanguard Balanced Fund
Exxon, Apple, Chevron, GE, IBM

Owning more than one fund like this is false security. If giant US firms stumble, your portfolio will not have assets that provide an offsetting balance. I wish there was a way to screen financial advisors for good judgment. Yes, meet with an advisor and ask questions. But, don't let the guy screw things up.

Tom's Tip:

Index funds provide average market risk. Combine index funds of different types and with no overlapping assets to create a portfolio with below average risk.

The Right Way to Use a Financial Advisor

Use an advisor for what they do well. A good advisor can review your assets, earnings, and retirement goals and provide some good information. Just before retirement, they can tell you a withdrawal rate from savings so you don't outlive your money. They know all about IRAs and various tax deferred accounts. Regular checkups with an advisor may be useful for some people. Properly used, a professional advisor is a good resource for financial planning.

How do people go wrong? They turn over their assets to the advisor. At this point, the advisor has a conflict of interest. Your primary interest is to make your money grow. His primary interest is to earn a good living and your money makes that happen. Pay the advisor for advice and invest the money yourself. Make your intention clear from the very beginning. You're under no obligation to have the advisor manage your money or to pay anyone a percentage of your assets.

If you want an advisor, you're much better off with a fee-paid advisor (http://www.napfa.org/), who checks over your investments each year for a modest fixed fee. Be careful, some will try to charge a fee as a percent of your assets – this is not acceptable. Do not pay a percentage of your assets to anyone! Paying commissions on your own money is just plain foolish.

If you don't have much money, perhaps the advisor's fixed fee will equal the 1% commission fee. Well, money grows over time and so do bad habits. Pay the fixed fee and don't waste time comparing apples to oranges. In the long run, you'll be much better off investing your own money.

Educate yourself all the time, so when you meet with your financial planner or CPA he/she sees a smarter and more confident investor. If you use an advisor, they deserve fair compensation but not a piece of the action.

My Methods Won't Work with Managed Funds

To take advantage of the techniques I'll soon show you, you need to invest in index funds. Low expenses and average market risk are required for my portfolios to work. Managed funds won't work because their style of investing often changes over time. Ownership of the fund changes, managers come and go and investing trends change causing management to shift direction.

This "style shift" means you never know how the fund's holdings are weighted relative to a benchmark index. Read any mutual fund annual report and the fund manager will say things like "we over-weighted the blah-blah-blah sector to take advantage of blah-blah-blah". The fund's concentration of assets changes year to year. This lack of consistency isn't helpful for creating a balanced mix of assets.

Get into Index Funds

There's no reason for you to invest in managed mutual funds unless you're an active, passionate investor who understands markets and enjoys research and actively managing your money.

Are you willing to regularly monitor the performance of your managed funds and compare them against industry benchmarks? Will you notice if the superstar fund manager leaves the company and your fund performance starts to falter? Will you pay attention if fund expenses creep up or if the fund changes its investment objectives? Do your read the fund prospectus or even know what they're talking about?

Don't buy managed funds unless you enjoy spending a lot of time on your investments and can do a great job. Managed funds don't outperform index funds over most five-year periods. They have higher costs and take on more risk.

With an index fund portfolio, you don't need a commission financial advisor skimming away 3% of your returns every year with high fees and lower performance. With an index fund portfolio, you get the average performance and risk inherent in the market. When certain types of index funds are combined in the right proportion, you get optimized costs, performance and risk.

The idea of good returns and low costs probably appeals to you. When I show you how to reduce or eliminate losing years, there won't be anyone big enough on Wall Street to stop you from moving into the realm of "long-term successful investor". But, what if your retirement plan has you locked into high expense, managed mutual funds? There is probably a way out.

How to Un-Trap Your Money

Many people contribute to a 401k plan or 403b plan with their employer. Often, the mutual fund company selected to handle employee contributions has a limited selection of funds or has high fees. Fees are money out of your pocket and must be avoided. Some employers offer several fund companies. Check out the returns of your company sponsored plans for the last ten years. Look at the returns and the expenses and compare them to my model portfolios and index funds. Maybe the plan does a great job of providing low cost solutions. If that's the case then be thankful and stay with a winner.

Most small employers are forced to select a fund company based on the free services it can provide. This way the employer doesn't have to do as much paperwork. The fund management company passes the costs through to the employee as fees. This is a bad arrangement for the worker. There are three ways to work an employer plan to your advantage.

Take Advantage of the Funds Network Feature

Some retirement plans allow investors to buy the funds of other companies through a "Funds Network". To find out, call up your plan's representative and ask if the feature is available. If it is, you'll continue to contribute to your employer's plan, but the money actually goes to buy shares in index funds. Take advantage of the funds network feature to lower costs and improve performance. Vanguard should be your first choice, due to its super low fee structure and tremendous choice of index funds.

Do a Rollover to Another Fund Company

If you've changed employers you can roll your money to a another company. In a 401k or 403b plan this is easy to do. Don't take a "Distribution" from your 401k fund. This can be a taxable event with penalties. A distribution is when the plan mails a check payable to you and you cash it. Don't do that! The money must be transferred from your employer plan directly to a Rollover IRA.

Open a Brokerage Account

Your plan may allow opening a brokerage account. In that case, you can purchase Exchange Traded Funds (ETF). The ETFs are identical to many index funds and are an excellent way to index. This will be explained in more detail later in the book.

If none of the above options are available, then don't contribute to the company retirement plan. Some will disagree with my opinion. I think you're better off paying taxes on the income and investing the after tax dollars in a Roth IRA where it can compound tax free. This frees you from the company plan and provides flexibility. Some large employers offer a generous matching investment up to a percentage of your income. In that case, the choice is more difficult.

5

Investments to Avoid

Cautions on Certain Investments

You may have a separate pile of cash set aside to invest. Perhaps you've been a good saver or received an inheritance or sold a house. This chapter is about where not to invest.

When an investment advisor sees a pile of cash they will attempt to get it invested in something that will earn them a commission. The bigger the commission, the worse it is for you. In a nutshell, stay away from anything you don't understand. If you understand nothing, then finish reading this book and invest in my Balanced Portfolio #2. Don't be ashamed about your lack of knowledge, because admitting the fact is a lot better than losing a lot of money.

You can adjust your portfolio later as your confidence grows. You should only invest in things you fully understand. If uncertain, discuss it with a CPA or a fee-paid financial advisor or an attorney. Don't hesitate to get advice before investing. I believe the following investments are not a good idea for most people.

Annuities

The next chapter discusses these products in some depth. For the vast majority of people, a variable or deferred annuity is a bad investment with high expenses, surrender charges and paltry returns. You can do much better elsewhere. A Fixed Annuity pays a fixed amount per month for life and may be suitable in some specific situations. Investing your money in one of my recommended portfolios is usually a better idea. Insurance companies are good at providing insurance and that's about all.

Banks

Most banks now offer investment products. Banks are worse than insurance companies when it comes to fees. They steer money into high expense mutual funds with sales charges. Never invest your money with a financial consultant who works for a bank.

Stockbrokers

These folks are the front line sales staff of the financial services industry. Entrusting them with your money is probably not a good idea. They may or may not provide good general advice; it's a crap-shoot. Their purpose of existence is to steer your cash into speculations and risky ventures. This job title goes by various names. If they work for a big brokerage firm or mega-bank, be on high alert. You'll probably be charged too much.

Revocable Living Trusts

A living trust is essentially a legal document that places assets under the control of an executor. At death, the trustee acts in a fiduciary role to administer the assets for the beneficiaries in accordance with the owner's wishes. Since it's 'revocable' it can be cancelled at any time. A living trust is useful in cases where there's a greater risk of physical incapacity. People who own lots of real estate or who have a complex estate may benefit. A living trust probably isn't appropriate for a younger, healthy person or someone with few assets.

People are told their estate can avoid probate if they get a trust. Probate isn't a big deal. A big fee is often charged to up a trust. They don't cut your taxes and some of the other supposed benefits are over-rated. It's not a replacement for a will. Current laws allow people to bequeath large amounts untaxed at death to their heirs. Before buying into this through a financial planner, see an attorney. It's unlikely the average person will ever need a trust

ASSET PROTECTION SEMINARS

There's a whole industry of insurance firms pitching these seminars to people over the age of 55. They offer to set up a free trust or provide financial advice. The seminars are often held at local restaurants and a free meal is provided. The real objective is to gather financial information about the attendees as a prelude to selling them annuities. More on that a bit later.

INDIVIDUAL STOCKS

Buying individual stocks will probably not be a market beating strategy unless you're a savvy investor or have valuable industry knowledge that provides an edge. If you receive stock options or profit sharing, avoid holding the bulk of your assets in your employer's stock. Regularly diversify your holdings. Don't let an investment advisor steer more than 10% of your assets into trading stocks. Even that is probably too much. Most people are far better off in an index mutual fund.

LADDERED BONDS

You'll hear people say "I don't worry about the markets; I'm in laddered bonds". This means all their money is in bonds with different maturity dates. Some of the bonds mature in three years and some in twenty. Thus they lock in short term and long-term interest rates.

Well, guess what. A portfolio invested 100% in bonds is not very smart. You'll do a bit better than inflation and will have safety, but you're guaranteed a low rate of return; hence a low withdrawal rate. The withdrawal rate is the percent of your portfolio you can take out each year without dangerously depleting your capital. If the draw down rate is too high you will outlive your money.

A 100% bond portfolio will work for wealthy people who want no risk. They can survive easily on a low rate of return. For the person of average means, laddered bonds will not provide an acceptable rate of return after inflation. A bond index fund is better than laddered bonds and only when it's part of a broader investment portfolio that includes various assets. Laddered bond strategies purchased through brokerages and advisors often have high fees.

Syndications, Hedge Funds, and Partnerships

As a class, all these investments are far too risky for any but the most sophisticated investors or the rich and careless. These products are sold to people as smart, high return strategies and usually over a free dinner at a fancy location with plenty of attentive staffers.

Promoters want money for making movies, gold mining, real estate development, energy exploration and other risky ventures. Don't waste your time unless you understand the business. They're only offering you the opportunity to invest because Wall Street isn't interested. The same holds true for initial public offerings of stock. Stay away.

Business Ventures of Friends and Relatives

About 50% of new businesses fail within five years. Loaning money to buy shares in a new venture likely means a 50% chance of losing your entire investment. 59% of new restaurants fail within three years and for franchises it's 57%. Of those businesses that survive, the rate of return on investor capital probably isn't very good.

I can understand trying to help your child get a start in life and providing some living expenses for a while. It's not wise to loan 30% of your savings so they can start a car dealership or a distributorship. A bank will lend if there's collateral plus a good business plan. You're asked for money because it's a risky business proposition with a good probability of total loss. <u>Never</u> put up your house as collateral for a child's business or for a large bail bond. Learn to say no and stand firm.

The best strategy is not to talk about your net worth with people and that may include the kids. The retirement money is yours. They can have what's left after the funeral.

DOING BUSINESS WITH FELONS

I'd be cautious about trusting a convicted felon with money or revealing information to one. People don't end up in prison because of bad luck. First offenders rarely serve prison time so a multi-year sentence or a history of several convictions should be a big tip-off. Most people in the prison system are retarded, mentally incompetent, or suffer from a severe antisocial personality disorder.

6

ANNUITIES

Annuities come in two forms: Fixed Annuity and Variable Annuity. Variable Annuities are either Immediate or Deferred. I'll discuss these broadly. There are many variations. It's always a good idea to consult with a tax attorney and do a lot of research before buying an annuity. The products are aggressively marketed because they bring in big profits and commissions for the financial services industry. A wrong decision can be an immense mistake for the investor.

Let me summarize by saying that annuities are generally a poor investment choice for people over 65. In my opinion, they're a bad choice for young people too. My conservative Balanced Portfolio #2 will provide better income than an annuity. I believe people should choose a conservative and sensible investment strategy over an annuity. Most rate quotes on annuities won't show the high fees and severe restrictions.

A salesman with advanced degrees and insurance industry credentials can lull you into complacency. If you feel uneasy or don't fully understand what you're being sold, it's Fear gently warning you to be cautious.

FIXED ANNUITIES

When you buy a Fixed Annuity, you give an insurance company a chunk of cash. In return, they promise to pay you a set amount for life or for a specific period of time. You get more money each month by taking a shorter payout period. A smaller monthly payout is received if the annuity is for life. It's even less if you add a spouse's lifetime. The allure of these products is the "guaranteed" monthly payment.

A defined benefit pension plan that you've contributed to over a working career is really a type of fixed annuity. At retirement, it pays a fixed amount each month as long as you live or for a set period. It's best to just call it a pension if an employer provides it.

Most pensions have the option to allow the spouse to continue receiving a percentage of the benefits after the pensioner's death. Usually there's a modest reduction in monthly benefits. It's usually wise to include the spouse on the pension. This may not be necessary if there are other income sources or the spouse is likely to have a shorter life span.

Pensions are excellent and aren't a rip-off. That's because professionals act on behalf of the company and the employee to manage the money. Good performance of the invested assets equates to a lower required contribution rate for the company and a secure flow of funds for the employee. Thus, in a pension plan, the employer and the employee have the same financial objective.

The motivating factor for insurance companies offering annuities is quite different. They seek to maximize returns for the company over what they're contractually required to pay out to the annuitant. In addition, the salesman makes a big commission selling annuity products and this fee comes out of the investor's money.

A pension fund is highly motivated to keep the fund solvent and performing at a high level because this is mutually beneficial to the annuitant and the employer. The insurance company, on the other hand, offers a return just good enough to get your cash. The objective is to get a high spread between what they earn versus what they pay out.

A fixed annuity is a good financial decision only when immediate guaranteed cash flow is the most important factor. Peace of mind despite a lower lifetime return can be worth a lot.

Be Careful with Retirement Payouts

At retirement, employees are sometimes offered a choice of a cash payout or a monthly pension. For most retirees, the guaranteed monthly check is the safest path. There's no commission involved or sleight of hand and everybody is treated the same. Good providers of pensions are various government employers, union plans, and standard pensions offered by large employers.

Be very careful if you get a sales pitch from an insurance or annuity salesman when offered a payout choice. If you feel Fear warning you that he doesn't understand the spiel, it's best to visit a trusted financial advisor to get some good advice.

Remember, a fixed annuity is a promise to pay a stream of income in exchange for handing over a lump sum to the insurance company. The monthly check you receive depends on your age at the time you purchase the annuity. When you die, the income may continue to your spouse, but selecting this option means you'll get a lower payout over the life of the annuity. Annuity payments all depend on how the annuity is structured. With a fixed annuity, when the last beneficiary dies, the insurance company retains the cash paid in.

I don't believe buying fixed annuities at retirement from an insurance company is the correct action for most people. If you decide to accept a cash payout at retirement, roll the money into an IRA and invest it in a conservative portfolio. This will produce more lifetime income than buying an annuity with the payout.

FIXED ANNUITIES ARE ESPECIALLY BAD FOR YOUNG RETIREES

I don't see the benefit of buying a fixed annuity for a young person. A 60 year old will receive about 50% less per month on an annuity investment than a 75 year old. That's because the younger man has a remaining life expectancy of 18.4 years versus 9.2 years for the older man.

Let's say you invest $100,000 in an annuity and receive $600 per month. The $7,200 a year you receive is not a 7.2% return on investment. It's actually much lower because there's no principal returned when the annuity ends; i.e. you die.

Some younger retirees may only care about getting a guaranteed monthly check as long as they live. They may figure, "Who cares if it's a low rate of return. I want that check in my mailbox for the next 20 years." Think again. Fixed annuities are not adjusted for inflation.

If you live another 20 years and inflation averages 2.5% yearly, the real value of your spending power from the annuity declines rapidly. After 10 years the annuity will buy 25% less in real money (10 x 2.5% = 25%). After twenty years the real purchasing power drops 50% (20 x 2.5% = 50%). What about your spouse if he or she is younger than you? Can they survive on what assets remain?

The insurance industry has countered by offering annuity products with a form of "indexing" to increase the payout in later years. It just means you get less in the earlier years. If you invested the money in one of my balanced portfolios, you'll do better than an annuity and will have the principal left to bequeath to an heir. It should be obvious that buying a fixed annuity is not wise for a younger person because fixed income loses to inflation. The power of compounding is the solution and that requires investing. A check in the mailbox each month is appealing, but maybe working for a while to gain some supplemental income is a better idea.

Fixed annuities offer the advantage of a guaranteed income stream. This comes at a high cost. The only reason you're offered an annuity is because the insurance company figures it can make money on your money after paying you. Actually, they know they'll make money, because it's all based on actuarial tables predicting likely longevity and conservative market return assumptions.

VARIABLE ANNUITIES

These products are sold to people as a way to build wealth through tax deferral. They come in many forms. A variable annuity is a contract between you and an insurance company, under which the insurer agrees to make periodic payments to you. You purchase a variable annuity contract by making either a single purchase payment or a series of purchase payments. The Securities and Exchange Commission provides a good explanation on their web site. http://www.sec.gov/investor/pubs/varannty.htm

A variable annuity offers a range of investment options. The value of your investment as a variable annuity owner will vary depending on the performance of the investment options you choose. The investment options for a variable annuity are typically mutual funds that invest in stocks, bonds, money market instruments, or some combination of the three. Although variable annuities are typically invested in mutual funds, variable annuities differ from mutual funds in several important ways.

First, variable annuities let you receive periodic payments for the rest of your life (or the life of your spouse or any other person you designate). This feature offers protection against the possibility that, after you retire, you will outlive your assets. Second, variable annuities have a death benefit. If you die before the insurer has started making payments to you, your beneficiary is guaranteed to receive a specified amount – typically at least the amount of your purchase payments. Your beneficiary will get a benefit from this feature if, at the time of your death, your account value is less than the guaranteed amount. Third, variable annuities are tax-deferred.

Variable annuities are designed to be long-term investments, to meet retirement and other long-range goals. Variable annuities are not suitable for meeting short-term goals because substantial taxes and insurance company charges may apply if you withdraw your money early. Variable annuities also involve investment risks, just as mutual funds do

If the payouts start immediately it's called an Immediate Annuity. If the money is invested and paid out later, it's called a Deferred Annuity. The combination of "tax deferral" and "safety of principal" is the hook used to snag the investor. Here's what is really going on.

Most variable annuities are just a mutual fund with a near meaningless insurance layer attached. At a future date you can withdraw your money. Yes, the assets can "grow" tax deferred but look at the downsides. Buying one incurs a front-end sales charge and hefty annual fees. After purchase, they offer poor liquidity, which means it's costly to change the investment mix. Try to get out early and you incur a "surrender charge" perhaps for up to 8 years. Then there's the 10% tax penalty if the money is withdrawn before age 59 ½. Finally, the earnings income distributed from the annuity is taxed as ordinary income instead of the much lower rate of capital gains from a regular mutual fund.

If the owner dies, the heirs do not receive a "step-up basis" on the inherited money. This means the heirs have to pay taxes on the profits. Regular stocks and mutual funds, not in an annuity, benefit from a step-up in tax basis.

Money in an IRA or other retirement plan is already tax deferred and gains nothing from a move to a variable annuity. Investors should maximize contributions to their IRA or other tax advantaged plan before even considering an annuity.

Knowledgeable investors don't buy variable annuities but the financial services industry sure knows how to sell them. In 2010 they sold $136 billion in variable annuities and well over a trillion in assets are now trapped in them. Annual fees run 4% per year. These products are marketed so hard and are so confusing that the National Association of Security Dealers issued an Investor Alert to warn of the dangers.

I said earlier to be careful if your retirement dollars in an employer retirement plan will be managed by an insurance company. Uninformed investors may think they're buying a mutual fund when it's really a deferred annuity. Be certain you're buying into a mutual fund and not an annuity product. High fees and insurance jargon are the tip off. If you don't understand it, then don't buy it.

Insurance is a profitable business. The annuity products sold by financial advisors on behalf of insurance companies are usually a bad deal for the investor. The insurance industry sells annuity products because they know they can invest the money and earn more than they'll pay out. You can do much better investing your own money, if you manage the risk. It isn't hard to do and I'll show you how. That's why you're reading this book!

I can't stress enough that you should research annuities before buying into any of the products. You can learn about fixed and variable annuities by getting a book at the library. Consult a tax/ estate attorney if you need estate planning or a will. They can provide better objective advice than a commission financial advisor. This book is not a substitute for good legal advice.

Lawyers should charge a fixed fee and not a commission. A competent lawyer is a valuable asset. I stress the word 'competent' because there are bad ones too. You have to be careful nowadays because some CPAs and attorneys now act as financial advisors. They're in the business to make money off your assets rather than provide the service of giving good advice. Ask them directly if they make a commission by selling you a service or product. If the answer is yes then go to someone else. Don't be shy. This conflict of interest can be very costly.

SHOULD ANYONE BUY AN ANNUITY?

Some financial advisors push hard to steer old people into inappropriate annuities because they succumb easily to fear. The advisor receives a huge commission on the contract and the product may poorly serve the client. That's especially true of deferred annuities. I can't stress enough that older people with declining abilities or financial problems need the assistance of an attorney knowledgeable about eldercare issues. Steer older people first to a specialist lawyer and not to an insurance company salesman.

EXCEPTIONS TO THE RULE OF AVOIDING ANNUITY PRODUCTS

Case 1: An older retiree hasn't enough money to live on. Let's say a 75-year-old man has $100,000. Even if he invests and earns 8% on the money, that's only $8,000 a year or $665 a month. A Fixed Annuity for life will pay more per month starting immediately. The amount of the annuity is based on a person's actuarial expected life span. In the case of our 75 year old man, that remaining life span is 9.2 years. If the extra monthly income is important, then the annuity is a good idea. If he lives to 99, he beats the insurance company at its own game because the annuity continues until death. Of course, at death, the insurance company keeps the remaining cash.

Case 2: Another reason to maybe buy an annuity is to prevent the government from grabbing assets if a spouse must go into a nursing home. Medicare will only start paying the nursing home bills when the spousal assets over a certain small limit are exhausted. This is often a disaster scenario for the remaining spouse. In this case, an annuity may be a wise estate planning tool because the annuity may be exempt from the Medicare asset limit. You need good advice from a specialized attorney before buying one. There are other capital protecting actions you can take to prevent your state or the Feds from grabbing all the loot.

My mother faced this issue when my father had Alzheimer's. Our attorney quickly put her house into a Life Estate and made sure she had financial power of attorney. With a Life Estate, the house is deeded to the kids but the parent can live there for life and even rent out the place. The parent cannot be forced to move. In our state, the house was then exempt from the limit on spousal assets. When my mother dies, the family gets the house on a stepped-up tax basis. Meanwhile, she lives securely in her own home.

Absolutely see an attorney if faced with end of life or nursing home issues. Just make sure you get initial advice from an attorney who doesn't sell annuities.

Case 3: Spendthrift, wastrel, and profligate all mean the same thing – a person who spends wastefully. Modern America has its share of them. This group should consider an annuity if they come into a large sum of cash. These folks show a lifetime pattern of making bad financial decisions. They may be smart people in other areas but not with money. There's a 90% chance this doesn't include you if you're reading this book and have made it this far. It's ok to be uneducated about money because, if you're eager to learn, you will. You're half my audience, good buddy, and that's why I wrote this book. My concern is people who don't get it and never will. Ask yourself these questions and be honest.

Am I unable to save despite having plenty to live on?

Do I frequently set back my financial goals by giving away money to relatives or friends?

Do I feel guilt saying no to salesmen, the kids, my church or charities?

Do I have a history of addiction to gambling, drugs or conspicuous, ego-driven spending?

Am I a compulsive shop-a-holic with closets full of unnecessary purchases?

Do I consistently overspend far beyond what is reasonable for my income?

Do I refinance the house to make unnecessary consumer purchases?

I'm not criticizing anyone who loves spending money on luxuries. The concern is living beyond your means and having no wealth set aside for later life. This includes disregarding the future welfare of a life partner and other family members.

Young and broke is understandable. Young people often have a hard time saving, because they need so many things to get started in life. Steady work and good sense brings success all the time despite very humble beginnings. However, by the time a person is 45, it becomes fairly clear that the spending situation is either improving or getting worse. I'm not asking you to make a moral judgment, but to acknowledge based on facts and historical observation, whether things are improving or staying the same. Counseling can help to examine habit patterns and identify ways to act constructively. Good advice from family and the kind intentions of friends usually won't work, because it's taken as an intrusion or an insult.

Compulsive behavior is disastrous for money management. If you have a personality with extreme self-control problems or compulsions, then put down this book and buy a fixed annuity. This book will not help you.

Spouses of people with self-control problems are another high-risk group. A person may want to save and plan but is married to someone who has to spend on cars, toys, vacations, or expensive gifts. They'll pester and use guilt or construct elaborate scenarios to justify a purchase in order to wear down their partner until they agree to release some money. This goes on repeatedly and makes it impossible to save for long-term goals like retirement. For many married people, common goals can emerge over time and a wonderful balance can result. Sadly, married people often move in opposite directions and great stress ensues.

Financial problems are the number one cause of divorce. Hiding a significant amount of money from your spouse probably won't work because, during divorce, full disclosure of assets must be made. Lawyers can easily do asset searches to find bank accounts.

It's best to recognize a marital mistake early and deal with it. This is always difficult if children are involved. Another option is to funnel the cash into an IRA, which can't be touched by the partner. Check with a lawyer for ways to protect spousal property from a spendthrift. A type of trust may be a better option than an annuity.

What if You Already Own an Annuity?

Find out the average yearly costs of your annuity product. What are the surrender charges? Don't expect the insurance company to give you clear information. You'll have to push hard to find out how much is being charged in expenses and fees each year. It's probably excessive. The fees and charges of some deferred annuities are so high they can cancel out the meager benefits of the tax deferral they're supposed to provide.

One option is to move your money into a lower cost annuity. Contact the Vanguard Group for help in understanding your options. They offer well priced products if you want to transfer your annuity. Vanguard offers variable annuities with low management fees and expense charges. Their average yearly cost is only 0.57% compared to the industry average of 2.39%. On every $100,000 you invest, excessive charges can cost $1,800 a year.

You can do a 1035 Exchange to move your annuity assets tax-free from your existing institution to Vanguard. The money lost on the front-end sales charges can't be recovered but you can stop the yearly expense hemorrhage from stealing away your assets.

7

BAD ADVICE

The calamity of the 2000-2002 stock market crash, the 2007 housing crash and the 2008 stock crash crushed many investors. Retirements were delayed and many swore they'd never invest in stocks again. Yet, most are back in the market and will undoubtedly suffer the same fate in the future. This will occur because small investors haven't been shown simple ways to safely grow their money.

The people who work the jobs that sustain this nation, teach our kids and who serve on the front lines of our military deserve good information so they can retire comfortably. The problem is many people don't save because they don't believe they can win.

The whole subject of personal finance and investing has become very confusing to the average person. An entire financial media industry now exists on TV and the Internet. Celebrity commentators spout technical information and support it with colorful charts. Attractive hosts provide fawning admiration for this keen insight. The commercials that support this programming push the services of major Wall Street firms.

You can't blame people for believing the average guy has no chance trying to succeed without paying these "geniuses" for advice. Since it's not in the interest of these for-profit firms to educate the public, you can be sure the truth won't be coming from Wall Street. Fact is, the financial media world is full of hype. It's a myth that their services are essential for success. You're better off without them.

Though people may conclude that the financial services industry holds all the good cards, it's just not true. The problem is small investors aren't aware they are playing in a rigged card game. All they have to do is get up and move to another table.

The Cult of Experts

I recently read a newspaper article by a syndicated financial columnist and financial advisor. He tells his clients to put 80% of their money in US stocks and 20% in foreign stocks. That's 100% stock exposure. His reasoning is "massive amounts of academic research show that, over long periods (10 years or more), stocks have earned more than bonds". Yes, stocks earn more than bonds over most periods of time, but not one pension fund in America invests this way. They all hold some bonds. Any financial pro with common sense can tell you this guy's plan is loaded with risk.

This 100% stock portfolio is typical of the bad advice offered by self-interested financial planners. There are two problems with it. First, the stock market could fall a lot just before you retire and ruin your financial plan. Second, you can get close to the same return as his 100% stock portfolio and with a lot less risk. That may seem hard to believe but you'll see it's true.

If your sole objective is the highest possible return with no regard to risk, then concentrating your money in stocks may seem like the way to go. I don't advise that approach to even young people. Here's why.

Average yearly returns have many ups and downs. What looks good over many years doesn't reflect the situation at every point in time. When a person needs access to their money the most, the markets may be in a trough and values greatly reduced. This is actually quite likely to happen because people usually need to tap their savings during deep economic downswings. At these times, there are many layoffs and jobs are hard to find. These bad economic periods often coincide with weak stock prices. Financial planners who advise a 100% stock approach poorly serve their clients. People live in the real world and not in one of long-term averages.

The celebrity financial advisor goes on to say that you should never switch stock funds. "Choose your funds and stick with them as though they're tattooed to your arm." He's really saying: don't sell the high fee funds I'm earning a commission on. He then says that, after your pot of money has grown, you can start to diversify away from stocks. "Only a meeting with your personal financial advisor can provide effective answers for you". In other words, keep paying my fees and in some future year we'll change things, but don't think for yourself in the meantime. Friends, this nationally syndicated columnist blatantly gives advice that I believe puts your assets at high risk. If planners publicly give such advice, then imagine what they might suggest behind closed doors.

By the time you finish this book, there will be no doubt in your mind that the above advice is not a good idea and that you can do better ignoring this kind of self-serving foolishness. Investing is not difficult if you know the basics. Here's something you need to know. All asset classes have peaks and troughs in valuation. The most money is made by buying at cyclical lows and selling near the top. You should be trading the cycle whether it's stocks, bonds or gold.

The media conglomerates and their financial services industry advertisers support the cult of experts. Let's have some fun and pick them apart a bit.

The Mass Media has Little Useful Information

Massive conglomerates with vast entertainment company holdings own the major news media and TV networks. For example, Disney owns ABC, Comcast owns NBC and Time Warner owns CNN. Their drive for ratings is behind the cult of celebrity and dumb-downed editorial standards. The decline in newspapers plus the ownership of news outlets by major media companies has resulted in reduced investigative news staff and weak research. It's never been easier for politicians and Wall Street to bamboozle the public.

This became obvious when the major news media neglected to investigate government lies and distortions leading up to the Iraq war despite ample warnings from national security insiders. Reporters said they were afraid for their jobs if the public saw them as "unpatriotic". Can you imagine Walter Cronkite using that as an excuse? I have no doubt that the media company moguls were afraid the truth would antagonize the public and hurt ratings.

Much of what we hear and view on TV financial programs is useless information. On financial talk shows, I hear discussions about "buy and sell points", "price support levels" and "momentum". One show has a guy with rolled up shirt sleeves accepting calls from listeners and giving a machine-gun analysis of stock price charts or a company's business prospects. It sounds like keen insight. This is actually Ouija Board investing. These shows are simply entertainment.

There are legions of fans that tune in daily to celebrity financial entertainers to get their opinion on stocks and market trends. It's a lucrative gig, but I don't see how an investor can make a nickel from any of it. It's a combination of statistics, blather and half-truths fed to the naïve over the airways. During market corrections, their panic inducing hyperbole is downright dangerous to your portfolio.

Then, there are those laughable magazine articles shouting out stories like 'The 10 Top Stocks to Buy Now'. Magazine cover recommendations are often articles by young staff writers with lots of ideas but little experience in actual investing. Personally, I rarely pay any attention to TV financial news or most mass-market financial magazines. The articles may be interesting, but the facts they report are already priced into the markets.

Don't Listen to Wall Street

Articles in magazines and the stuff on TV is hit and miss – and often terrible. Here are some general guidelines when it comes to free advice about the stock market.

Historically, mathematically, and factually, professional mutual fund managers can't consistently beat the indexes to which their funds are benchmarked. What then is their opinion worth on interest rates, world financial policy trends or any other topic?

These folks are interesting conversationalists but virtually nothing they say will make money for you.

Here's a fact. The average mutual fund manager may have a graduate MBA but not necessarily better common sense than you. He gets paid a lot of money because his industry has you convinced he's an expert. He may be an expert on many things, but not on outperforming the stock market and that's all that really matters to you. If he has a Finance MBA, he already knows about indexes and realizes he has a poor chance of beating them over time.

I wish it was that benign but it's not. A high percentage of money managers actually believe and act on superstitious methods of timing the financial markets. And worse, it's done with investor money. Later in this book, I will elaborate on some of these practices.

People who understand the stock market know it's "forward looking". That means it quickly discounts the probability, or likelihood, of something happening in the future. Like I said before, what's known is already 'priced' into the market. What might happen is also priced to a great extent. If an investor doesn't have an edge, or special knowledge, then it's nearly impossible to beat the market averages over time.

Wall Street firms want investors to think they can provide an edge over others. The big firms are always releasing their research on various topics like interest rates and stock sector themes. Ask yourself this question: "If what they're offering to the small investor had any value for making money then why would they give it to me?" Answer: They want you to think they know something useful so you'll give them some cash. Of course, they never tell you when to sell thus losing money is always your fault. They get fees and you get screwed. That, my friend, is a pattern you'll see over and over.

THE RICH ARE FEARFUL TOO

I recently read an article about a TV financial advice giver who said she was worth $25 million. She has only about $1 million in the stock market because that way she won't worry about losing money. The rest is invested in low return municipal bonds. Her behavior may strike some as hypocritical but I didn't see it that way. It's typical of the rich. They have enough income from a business or inheritance so that investing money in stocks isn't necessary. Stock market crashes don't affect the rich much at all.

Some wealthy people have much of their money tied up in business assets, which is a high-risk situation. For them, avoiding more investment risk is the smart thing to do. Our wealthy advisor above is acting rationally from her perspective and being honest about it. She has more than she can ever spend and excellent yearly cash flow.

This story does point out a remarkable fact. Even the very wealthy worry about money and are unsure they can succeed at investing. They suffer from the same fears as you and are as misled and confused by the financial services industry as anyone else. They, however, are in a situation where they can chose to avoid it. You can't.

It's good to have Fear tugging at your sleeve. The easy way out for the rich is risk avoidance, but for you, it must be risk management. Small investors invest in the markets because they don't have a huge pile of cash and must rely on steady savings and growth of capital to provide a pot large enough to retire on.

Proper money management is more difficult for workers than for the rich. As such, workers understandably worry about it more and are more prone to making life-altering mistakes if they act on bad information. Let's examine this idea because it's critical. <u>I have to get you to understand your situation and prove it to you or you won't catch the life-line I intend to toss out.</u> The primary fact is that bad information is everywhere and you mustn't act on it.

It's All Priced

Did you get what I said in the preceding paragraphs? I'll repeat. The big players in the financial community already know anything reported in the general news media. The financial markets have already adjusted to it. If you act on their news, it's not a good market bet. This is why panicking and moving your money around after hearing bad news is detrimental to successful investing. There's a corollary to this logic equation. If what you hear from public sources is already 'priced', then the only information you can justifiably act on is that which others don't already know.

To make market-beating bets, you need some inside information or must have some knowledge that most other investors don't possess.

1. You must be a well-placed person who knows in advance about a major corporate move or changes in governmental policy.

2. You must have a keen understanding of a specific industry.

3. You need a way to time the markets in a way that others don't use.

This leads to a simple conclusion. It's a waste of time and probably a money loser for you to invest in individual stocks. You don't know anything unique. Buying stocks based on PE ratios, cash flow, momentum, and charting techniques is a money losing waste of time. What you know is old news and millions of others are already doing it and having mediocre success at best. Most people who make a big score are simply lucky.

If you don't believe me, then try this. Go to Yahoo Finance (finance.yahoo.com) or visit a brokerage office and watch the quotes stream across the screen. What you're witnessing are big trades by mutual funds, speculators and giant brokerages all acting immediately on company news. Automated computer programs then buy and sell based on changing spreads between stock prices.

You can't consistently make money with old information from financial publications, the TV news or the Internet. It doesn't work because the news is already priced before it hits your local newspaper or home computer. You may get lucky on one stock but you'll lose on another. If that's true, and I'm sure it is, then what should the investor do if they can't afford to lose?

The only logical action is to take a market neutral position at all times. Be in broad asset classes so that, wherever money flows, you get a piece of the action. It's critical to understand that you can know little and still be a very successful investor. You just have to be in the right mix of assets.

As world wealth expands, more money comes into the system. You don't need to know where it's going. Just stand there and get paid. It's that simple. If money leaves the system suddenly due to a financial panic, you may not get paid, but you won't lose a lot either. That's because you'll also own the other asset that benefits from fear.

8

You Can Beat the Pros

Balancing assets in a portfolio is called Asset Allocation and it is used by every pension fund in the world. These funds must survive to pay off their contributors. If they don't, a company or the government is on the hook to make up the difference. For that reason, pension funds are closely watched by auditors to ensure prudent investment management.

Pension funds are staffed by smart and experienced managers. Guess what – they plan for consistent, long-term returns on their money. They hold a balanced mix of assets, carefully manage risk and costs and never chase fads. If you'd duplicate what they did you'd get same returns. Here's the good news. For the little guy, it's even easier. You can allocate a portfolio in ways they can't, because pension and mutual funds are forced by investment guidelines and charters to pursue a certain approach. Some are just too big to have much flexibility. That's why 60% of them can't beat the market indexes in any one year and virtually none do over longer periods of time.

The reason small investors rarely match the returns of pension funds is because of the high fees extracted by Wall Street, the banks and financial advisors. The name of their game is fees and commissions. Nobody discusses how to build a portfolio that serves to protect against big losses while delivering good returns. Instead, small investors pay for handholding and invest in assets with high expenses that are prone to underperform a properly balanced index fund portfolio. Furthermore, the assets are subject to collapse during a market crash or a deep recession.

The terms 'diversification" and "asset allocation" are widely abused by the financial services industry. They'll tell you that their mutual funds are diversified. They'll say their fund is 'balanced' with stocks and bonds thus implying it's diversified and safe. Like most everything else they say, it's somewhat true.

Below is the giant Fidelity Magellan fund. It's assets are 100% in stocks. I've compared it to the S&P500 Index from 2001 to 2010. Clearly, the fund's performance during the market crashes shows it's susceptible to big losses. A conservative investor wouldn't want to hold just this fund.

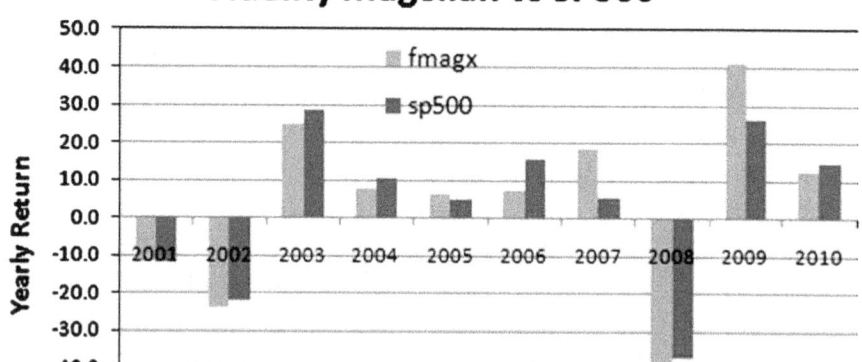

2001-2010 (10 yrs)	Fidelity Magellan	S&P500 Index
Avg. Yearly Return	3.3%	3.5%
Losing Years	3	3
Worst Year	-49.4%	-37.0%
Growth of $10,000	$9,800	$11,400

Over ten years, Magellan has underperformed the S&P500 index. It also lost more money during the 2001-2002 and 2008 stock market crashes than the index. An investor would have earned 16% more money in a mutual fund that tracked the S&P500 Index.

Financial advisors always recommend that investors hold some bonds to create a more balanced portfolio. Let's look at the popular Fidelity Asset Manager-50%. It holds half stocks and half bonds. It's marketed as a balanced, asset allocation approach for conservative investors. I've compared it to a 50/50 mix of the S&P500 and the Vanguard Total Bond Market Index Fund.

Fidelity Asset Mgr vs Index Blend

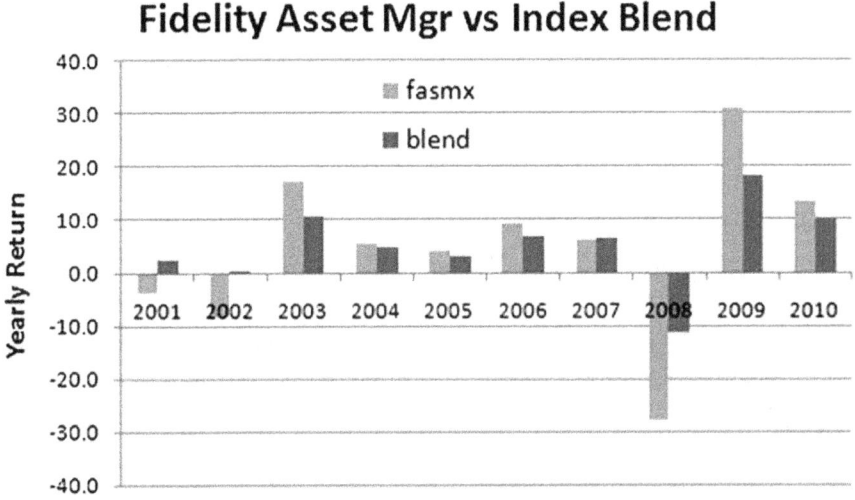

An investor would have done better owning the two index funds. Over ten years Asset Manager-50% has underperformed a 50/50 mix of the S&P500 and the Vanguard Total Bond Market Index. The index blend made 14% more money. Asset Manager also lost more money during the 2001-2002 and 2008 stock market crashes than the combined index funds.

2001-2010	Fidelity Asset Mgr	50/50 Mix Stock/Bond
Avg. Yearly Return	4.7%	5.1%
Losing Years	3	1
Worst Year	-27.8%	-11.4%
Growth of $10,000	$14,100	$16,100

I'm not out to pick on Fidelity. This sort of performance is typical of many managed funds over a ten-year period. Some funds may do better than a benchmark index for a while but the expense and performance advantage of the index fund always wins out. In addition, you never know which managed fund will do poorly or when.

There's an important message hidden in the data I've just presented. The years of 2001-2010 were a period of large stock market declines and recoveries. It was a time of wasteful war and reckless deficits. Still, the stock market was able to deliver a positive decade overall. Its rate of return was higher than the 2.4% average rate of inflation. It shows that money is best invested in asset classes instead of cash. The big problem is the volatility. In the pages ahead I'll show you how to reduce volatility by adding additional asset classes. Then I'll show you how to remove the negative return years of 2001, 2002 and 2008 from the S&P500.

The last ten years have been dismal for stock market investors. I suspect we face difficult conditions in the years ahead. The market shocks have caused many to reduce their stock exposure and invest more in the bond market. This will likely prove to be a bad decision with interest rates now so low. Unless there's a way to reduce risk and increase returns, people will abandon the stock market or put too much into bonds and lose bad when rates rise.

How to Beat the Market

There are two ways to beat the market. First, we can use passive investing. A small investor can create an effective mix of index funds that will outperform the multitude of Balanced Funds, Asset Allocation Funds or Retirement Target products offered by the big fund companies. This will also beat the best pension funds.

The second approach is active investing using market timing to avoid the steep downdrafts in the stock market. This approach is useful if it's simple.

Let's look first at passive investing using stock and bond index funds. For this example, I'll compare a traditional 60/40 stock/bond portfolio consisting of two Vanguard index funds to two of the best pension funds in America; California's CalPERS and Arizona's ASRS. The index funds are the Vanguard S&P500 index fund and the Vanguard Total Bond Market Index Fund. I'll also flip the stock/bond percentages and see how the 60/40 mix compares to more bonds in the 40/60 mix.

The table below shows the average annual returns for 5, 10, and 25 years.

Avg Returns	California CalPERS	Arizona ASRS	60/40 Index Mix	40/60 Index Mix
5 years %	3.9	3.4	6.6	6.1
10 years %	4.0	3.0	4.5	4.9
25 years %	9.5	10.4	10.0	9.2
# Losing Yrs	3	4	5	3
2008	-27.8	-7.6	-20.2	-11.8
2001-2002	-13.1	-14.9	-12.9	-2.4

The big pension funds have mega-billions in assets. They have an in-house investing staff plus they hire outside consultants to help manage their portfolios. They also own some real estate and exotic investments. I'm not impressed.

You can tie the best pension funds in America with two Vanguard index funds and with less risk. Over five and ten years the Vanguard index fund mix beat the two pension funds. Over twenty-five years the index mix did just as well. The Vanguard Total Bond Market Index fund is VBMFX. The Vanguard S&P500 fund is VFINX. The Vanguard ETF equivalents are BND and VOO.

This is absolute proof that you don't need a financial advisor to manage your money. All you have to do is rebalance the portfolio to 60/40 or 40/60 once a year. If, after one year, the stock percentage is above your target percentage then sell some stock and buy the bond ETF. Don't over manage it – just rebalance once a year. It really is that simple.

9

Manage Your Own Money

How the Deck is Stacked Against You

Many investment advisors have no financial incentive to consider your success over their own self-interest. They over-emphasize expensive stock and bond mutual funds and expose their clients to substantial risk during bad markets. Most investors are in mutual funds holding mostly large company stocks. Many don't have any small company stocks. Many of those big funds are little more than a basket of large company stocks that correlate tightly with the S&P500. Holding two or more large stock funds like that provides little in the way of diversification. You just get duplication. Adding mid-cap stocks doesn't help with the problem of excess correlation since they tend to move closely with the big companies.

Most investors have little exposure to high performing income assets like commercial real estate. Instead they're steered toward fixed income holdings in the form of ridiculous laddered bond products. This simply provides a pretense to charge high commissions. In short, the financial services industry has set up the average investor to be the patsy at a pickpocket convention.

In the next chapter, I'll show you how to build portfolios like those enjoyed by the savviest investors in the world. You can match the performance of the pros, plus pay nothing in fees and next to nothing in fund expenses.

It's all About Risk

The finance professors know all about risk and asset correlation. Correlation is the tendency of some asset classes to move with or opposite each other. Knowing about correlation will save your financial life. It's the difference between losing 30% in stocks during a bear market and breaking even. It's the reason why balanced and asset allocation mutual funds fail during crashes. This fact is real and operates every time the market experiences a severe correction. I'll explain asset correlation in detail in a forward chapter.

Wall Street knows that half of small investors will never "get it" and will always chase performance. They are too impatient and jump ship if their fund underperforms what another fund earned during a recent good year. The other half passively does whatever their advisor suggests. So, there's little incentive to offer financial products with more balanced returns.

Financial markets are cyclical and go through expansion and contraction phases. Sometimes, expansions can boost asset prices to crazy levels. Wall Street doesn't consider market crashes and severe declines very important because they make their money off of fees. To a person who can't afford to lose, it's financial life and death. To the mutual fund industry, given enough time, the markets will regain what they lost. This sort of thinking ignores what happens to the real people who don't have time to recover from deep bear markets.

Let me show you what happens to real people. Many investors in their 50's will never be able to retire because of the terrible market conditions over the years 2000-2010. Returns have been terrible. In 2001-2002 the S&P500 fell 34%. An investor with a $300,000 stock portfolio saw it drop to $198,000. She needed a 52% return to get even (1.52 x 198,000 = 300,000). By 2007 the market had risen 65%. Whew. She made it. Then the market got slammed by a 37% decline and her portfolio was down to $189,000. Now she needs a 58% return to get even. Meanwhile, inflation has averaged 2.1% each year or 21% over ten years. She really needs a 70% return to get even. Here in mid 2011, the global economy is starting to slump again. Risk is real and this is our reality.

The major concern of fund managers is beating their peers in the salary game, which means doing a bit better than the next guy. If their fund is down 20% and the average is down 22% they look like a winner in the industry. The major concern of commission advisors and annuity salesmen is maximizing their current income.

I have grave concerns with the optimistic projections for world economic growth. We face tremendous changes ahead due to globalization, oil depletion and changing global political alignments. Furthermore, millions of baby boomer workers are nearing retirement and will be net sellers of stocks. The past historical numbers for stock profits may be a poor guide to the future. The fastest future growth may be in the smallest firms that can adapt quickly to changing conditions.

Balance in a portfolio is more important than ever as we try to peer into the future. Experts can talk all they want, but their ruminations are conjecture and no one can confidently predict anything about how earnings will grow or how things will change over the next twenty years. I can guarantee you it will be much different from the past.

I'm sure there are some financial planners who can do an excellent job for their clients. The key problem is you won't know for sure about their recommendations until a time of financial crisis occurs and your portfolio is tested.

Uncertainty causes Fear to keep you awake at night and listening to the media experts during the day. Fear needs to know you're safe or he won't stop pulling on your sleeve and providing reasons to worry. The solution is to act with knowledge. If you can't afford to lose, then insist on using a sound strategy.

10
The Asset Classes

I've laid the groundwork for you and have explained why index funds are the most cost effective way to invest. I've explained that managed funds cannot be relied upon to provide consistent levels of risk. They can't outperform index funds over long periods of time. Let's discuss the popular investing method of Asset Allocation. Using a mix of asset classes to lower risk is a time honored investment tradition. In fact, a good mix can beat the 60/40 stock/bond mix with less volatility. I'll show you how this is done in this chapter.

Holding a mix of assets and rebalancing them once a year is an excellent idea. For many investors, this form of passive investing is all they need. It's perfectly acceptable to use it as your primary method of capital accumulation. I'll present a model portfolio that works well.

Later in the book, I'll show how to dramatically reduce investment risk while beating the indexes and any form of passive investing. Asset allocation is an important stop along the path.

Index Fund or ETF

First, let's distinguish between an index fund and an Exchange Traded Fund (ETF). There's been an explosion of ETF products from Barclays and Vanguard over the last several years. An ETF is an index fund, that's purchased on a stock exchange rather than as a mutual fund product. Many of Vanguard's index funds are also sold as an ETF. The ETF product has rock bottom expenses. Some ETFs are focused on narrow sectors of the market and I won't discuss those.

You need a brokerage account to buy these ETF products. In some instances, buying an ETF is a good idea if you can't buy into a Vanguard index fund directly. This would be useful for people who don't live in the US but want to use my portfolios. For that reason, I'll list the index fund and the corresponding ETF.

Some Major Indexed Asset Classes

There's nothing magical about an index fund. You just take a group of stocks or bonds and average the prices. The average price is the index. Half of the stocks or bonds will be priced above the index and half are below. The index is recalculated during the day and the new price is always being updated.

The S&P500 consists of 500 stocks. The Dow Jones Industrial Average has 30 stocks. A "commodity index" includes prices for gold, oil, gas, fibers, and many other products. The index is usually weighted. That means the biggest assets move the index price more than the smaller ones. For example, a change in the price of Wal-Mart impacts an index price much more than a price change in the smaller retailer Staples. As companies grow or falter, their impact on the index changes in direct proportion to their size. Periodically, companies are added or removed from the index.

In the stock arena, calling companies large and small is all relative. Companies in the Small Company Indexes are actively traded on the stock exchanges and employ many people and may even have international operations. They're small only relative to the giant firms. The Small Company stocks in the indexes are <u>not</u> tiny, risky, start up firms with no earnings and no history. These are legitimate operations and often are the up-and-comers of the business world. Of course, as a class, they don't have anything near the financial strength and broad presence of the giant firms. But, when you hold a lot of them in an index fund, they are no more risky than the S&P500 index.

The stock market is much more than giant companies and a good portfolio is much more than stocks.

Below are some popular indexes.

Short Term Bond Index These are bond securities with a duration of under 3 years. Very low risk. The safest short term bond funds invest mostly in US Treasury securities because there's no risk of default. This type of fund usually pays more interest than a money market but less than a longer term bond. You can even write checks on these funds.

Total Bond Market Index These are bonds with an average duration between 5 and 10 years. This index consists of every bond issued. It doesn't actually own every bond, but uses sampling techniques to effectively do the same thing. Bonds drop in value when interest rates rise because new bonds will pay a higher rate than the ones issued earlier. Bonds increase in value if interest rates fall. US government bonds dominate the index.

S&P500 This index consists of the 500 largest U.S. corporations. We usually invest in this group because it represents the backbone of the American financial system. You'll see this index discussed all the time.

Small Company Value Stocks This index is comprised of small U.S. stocks. They are called Value Stocks because they're small firms with lower price/earnings ratios. Effectively, that means the shares are selling at a discount to other small firms. Their prices bounce around more than the S&P500. The important thing is the prices don't generally move in the same direction as the big firms. This is important for getting a good mix of assets.

International Stocks This is an index of foreign stocks and includes companies in established and developing markets. Foreign companies are important to hold. Although this index often moves with the S&P500, it offers a critical quality we can't ignore –

currency diversification. If the dollar declines, these stocks move up. Thus, they provide not just growth, but protection against currency swings. By owning an International Stock Index, you essentially own a piece of every stock in the world and all the different currencies too.

Commodity Futures Index Fund This is an index of "commodity futures". A "future" is a contract to buy or sell a commodity at a future date. A commodity fund doesn't own the actual physical products or raw materials. It doesn't own the stocks of commodity producing companies. The fund buys contracts in the futures market on metals, grains, oil, and other physical materials. Commodities aren't a risky asset class if you own the index. They are risky if you're speculating on pork bellies or some minor segment of this market. Commodity futures don't move with stocks or bonds.

Real Estate Investment Trusts This is an index fund that holds stock shares of companies in the real estate business. It's abbreviated REIT. The companies own shopping centers, office buildings, apartments, and other income producing real estate assets. REITs are required by US law to pay out 90% of their profits to shareholders in the form of dividends. In many ways, a REIT is like a cross between a stock and a bond. Surprisingly, this index is not affected greatly by swings in interest rates. There are several reasons, but consider this. When rates go up, many people can't afford homes and so they rent apartments. Thus, apartment rents may rise due to increased demand while residential housing declines. Real estate is a broad market and diverse. Other nations are increasingly creating REIT-like share classes.

The next chart shows the historical returns of the selected asset classes and gold over the last thirty years. I discuss gold in its own chapter later in the book.

Index Asset Class	Average Returns				Losing Years	Worst Year
	30 Yrs	20 Yrs	10 Yrs	5 Yrs		
International Stocks	12.2	8.0	10.1	8.5	7	-43.4
S&P500	12.4	9.5	4.8	5.1	5	-37.0
Small Company Value	14.2	13.1	10.3	8.0	8	-28.9
US Bonds	8.9	6.2	5.0	5.7	2	-2.3
Short Term Bond	7.1	5.2	3.7	4.8	0	0.4
Money Market	4.6	3.0	1.6	2.1	0	0.0
Gold	4.7	7.8	18.3	24.4	12	-18.3
REIT	12.0	12.0	12.6	7.9	4	-37.0
Commodity Futures	8.2	7.8	10.0	8.3	6	-43.3

The worst year for all the stock indexes, REITS and commodities was 2008. The worst year for gold was 1982. Bonds haven't had any huge down years over the last three decades. That's because interest rates have mostly fallen since 1980. More on this topic later.

WHY NO DOW JONES INDUSTRIAL INDEX?

The news reports always discuss how the "Dow" index did for the day. This is a poor index to use for building a portfolio. It uses an old method of weighting stocks so the very largest firms unbalance it.

WHY NO MIDDLE SIZED STOCKS?

In my list above you may notice I don't list a big sector of the market called "Mid Cap Stocks". These are medium sized firms. They're smaller than the S&P500 companies and larger than those in the Small Company Indexes. On Wall Street they use the terms "Small Cap" rather than Small Company, but for our purposes it means the same thing. The term "Cap" is short for capitalization and it refers to the dollar amount of all the shares of stock investors own in a company.

I don't use Mid Sized Company indexes because they correlate too closely with the giant companies. You'll learn about this topic of "correlation" soon. When the big companies hit a rough patch and drop in a correction (short term slump), we don't want all our asset classes to follow. In fact, when one slumps another may go up. This smoothes out the volatility which means the value of your portfolio won't jump around as much.

Why so Few Asset Classes?

Some of you may be thinking: How can only a handful of index funds be enough to use in a portfolio? Folks, this is all you need. Each stock index fund tracks hundreds of companies.

Our goal is to build a high performing portfolio without using managed funds. Index funds are called "passive" investments because they aren't managed. Instead, they perfectly reflect an average. We use passive funds and don't pretend we can guess how a certain stock or bond will perform next year. It can't be done despite what Wall Street or talk radio "experts" suggest. This simple, time-proven strategy works, but only if the indexed assets are properly balanced together. In the next chapter, I'll explain how to avoid investment disasters. All that's needed are a few easy tweaks to create the right mix of assets.

11

THE SECRET OF SAFER INVESTING

WHAT FINANCIAL FIRMS DON'T TELL YOU

Financial firms that market index funds rarely discuss the dangers of holding various funds that move together in price. There's two reasons they don't discuss correlation. First, they won't tell you how to build a portfolio, because they know little about you and don't want to get sued if you misunderstand what they say. Second, the explanation requires discussing some statistics and they can't have experts of this caliber staffing the phones. Instead, some firms try to find some balance by steering you toward "Life-Cycle" funds.

These funds actually just shift around the percentage of stocks and bonds depending on your age and years to retirement. An automated approach like that is a step in the right direction, but rather crude. It's just another example of Wall Street over-selling a simple idea and implying it does a good job of managing risk.

YOU NEED A BROAD ASSET MIX

You don't need to know the math about investing but you do need to avoid too much of one type of asset. I'll provide the basic math and will explain why mixing assets is important. I know some people will need to see proof – and they deserve proof.

Many investors buy index funds, but end up holding a bunch of funds that move together. They get the low costs, but they miss out on the balance and diversification. A low risk index fund portfolio must avoid market segments that move together. Otherwise, during downturns, you'll be hurt badly.

Be Careful What You Index

The first index fund didn't appear until 1975. Index investing didn't become popular for another twenty years. The last ten years have seen an explosion in the number of index funds and ETF products.

The stock market can be sliced and diced into various segments and an index can be created for just about anything. In fact, the big financial firms have created many indexes and financial products, but investors have little understanding of the correct ways to mix them properly. Indexing is popular right now, but many types of index funds are much too narrow or risky for our purposes.

You can index financial stocks, health care, technology, and so forth. Some new index/ETF products cover areas of the market like dividend paying firms. These types of index funds are not useful because narrow market sectors make crummy indexes for the average investor.

For example, the S&P500 index has a lot of overlap with an index of dividend paying stocks called iShares Dow Jones Select Dividend Index (DVY). In addition, DVY consists of about 35% financial stocks. Most investors wouldn't be aware of that important fact. They'd find out very fast if interest rates rose and financial stocks slumped. Financial firms are sensitive to rate changes.

It's accurate to say that holding ETFs and index funds focused on narrow market sectors like technology, health care, and financials is not appropriate for most investors trying to build a balanced portfolio. In fact, the reason so many people lose enormous portions of their assets during market crashes is because they're invested in narrow sectors of the market. For an investor who can't afford to lose, this is always the wrong thing to do!

The positive thing about index funds is that it's very easy to mix them with no overlap. A portfolio I'll show you lost money during the 2008 market crash but much less than a pure stock portfolio. It's imperative that you understand the concept of why over-concentration of assets increases risk.

A Crash Course in Finance Statistics

When I was in business school, I really liked statistics. When I started working in the "real world" there were few places to use it for practical purposes. The world of commerce is a messy place for a businessman because competition, government, and people problems push things off track and then back on. The same goes for investors who are tossed around by the confusing array of financial products, index funds and conflicting advice provided by experts and the media.

Statistics can be interesting and maybe even fun to some people, but factoids about long-term returns are meaningless when you're 70. You can't wait for the statistical averages to revert to the average because you can't afford to lose.

Correlation

The tendency of indexes to move together or apart over long periods of time is called "correlation" in statistics. For example, if the price of cars always goes up when steel goes up then you have high correlation between car prices and steel prices. On the other hand, rising rubber prices may not push up car prices. Tires aren't as big a cost factor as steel in cars. There is low correlation between rubber prices and car prices. Commodity prices and the price of a finished product often don't move together closely.

Falling gasoline prices may increase business activity at regional theme parks because more people can now afford to drive there. In that case, we have "negative correlation" between gas prices and theme park profits. There is correlation but it's reversed. As gas prices fall, theme park sales may increase.

Many times there is "no correlation". An increase in the price of copper doesn't affect the price of garlic grown in California.

Now, consider the case of a street vendor in Seattle. On cold and rainy days, she will sell a lot of hot coffee. On warm and sunny days, she'll sell more frozen treats. There's positive and negative correlation between temperatures and various edible products.

A smart street vendor carries products to take advantage of the weather. A smart investor has a portfolio to take advantage of the asset classes as they move in and out of favor.

Asset Correlation

It's the same principle between different sized firms. Small companies are affected more by local labor and material costs than the big firms with a global reach. On the other hand, small firms are quicker to change suppliers and even their entire product line. They adapt quicker to situations. The profits of small company stocks are more susceptible to market changes than big firms. This shows up statistically in the trend of their year-to-year profits and losses, which are more variable than those of large firms.

It's possible to compare different indexes over the years and determine if they move together or apart. All the different asset classes I previously listed are in a range from low correlation to high correlation with each other. Some have no correlation. High correlation (positive or negative) means the assets are fairly certain to move together. No correlation means, if one asset moves, it's impossible to predict what another will do. Low correlation (positive or negative) means a change in one asset will have a minor impact on another.

The various segments of the stock market (S&P500, Small Company, and International) all move together, to some extent. International Stocks are significantly correlated with the S&P500 because large company stocks dominate both of the indexes. Small company stocks have much less correlation with either.

Bonds have high negative correlation with the S&P500 during market crashes when investors are fearful. During most months, some negative correlation exists but nothing like during a crash.

Commodities have poor correlation to stock prices and negative correlation with bonds. Gold is correlated somewhat with commodities, but not as much as you'd expect, because it's such a small part of the larger commodity index. Gold has unique qualities that keep in separate from other commodities.

Below is a table showing the correlation between some major asset classes. You don't have to spend much time on this but I've printed it for people who want to see the relationships. If this statistical talk makes your eyes glaze over, just skim it and move on. Anyway, the chart below covers a 30 year period.

Asset Correlation 1981 - 2010

	LTB	INTL	S&P	SCG	SCV	GOLD	REIT	STB	COMM
LTB	100%								
INTL	6%	100%							
S&P	30%	66%	100%						
SCG	12%	61%	83%	100%					
SCV	28%	41%	64%	71%	100%				
GOLD	-43%	26%	-10%	11%	-8%	100%			
REIT	3%	30%	40%	40%	69%	15%	100%		
STB	81%	2%	22%	0%	20%	-54%	-8%	100%	
COMM	-19%	47%	38%	45%	30%	57%	47%	-30%	100%
MM	46%	-2%	13%	-12%	6%	-66%	-6%	69%	-25%

LTB:	Long Term Bonds	Gold:	Gold
INTL:	International Stocks	REIT:	REIT Stocks
S&P:	S&P500 Index	STB:	Short Term Bonds
SCG:	Small Company Growth	COMM:	Commodity Futures
SCV:	Small Company Value	MM:	Money Market Funds

The table shows how returns on assets compare. This does not mean, for example, that a movement in the S&P500 <u>causes</u> another stock index to move up. Basically, it shows that if one asset moves up or down, then the other asset moves in the same or an opposite direction a certain percentage of the time. Various factors cause both assets to move. Assets that move together closely (positive or negative) are said to be "highly correlated".

Correlation is a tricky subject because the correlation between asset returns can be quite a bit different from one decade to the next. The Correlation Chart shouldn't be considered static and permanent rule. It indicates that, over long periods, asset returns move with or against other assets. We cannot forecast with certainty how the next five years of historical average relationships will play out.

The chart below shows the correlation table for the decade of the 1990s. There are some big differences from the 30 year correlation table.

	LTB	INTL	S&P	SCG	SCV	GOLD	REIT	STB	COMM
LTB	100%								
INTL	-7%	100%							
S&P	52%	40%	100%						
SCG	29%	54%	64%	100%					
SCV	49%	18%	54%	59%	100%				
GOLD	-23%	3%	-59%	-21%	-20%	100%			
REIT	26%	-34%	10%	4%	53%	24%	100%		
STB	98%	-17%	44%	29%	41%	-23%	23%	100%	
COMM	-41%	-1%	-23%	9%	-2%	49%	53%	-42%	100%
MM	22%	-56%	-1%	-20%	-43%	-12%	12%	34%	-3%

Asset Correlation 1990 - 1999

In the 90s there was more negative correlation between asset classes as shown by the negative values. History may be a useful guide but we can't use it to predict the future with any certainty. It is fair to say that a broad mix of assets will have correlations that offset each other over most time periods. Therefore, it's a good idea to look at the historical extremes of positive and negative correlation and to avoid concentrations of assets that move in lockstep with each other.

In the Correlation chart above, numbers above zero mean the assets move together to some extent in about the same proportion. Below zero it means they move in opposite directions in the same proportion. The correlation has to get around 50% or less than -50% to make a big difference in your portfolio.

When correlation is +75% that means asset A moves up the same percent as asset B most of the time. When correlation is -40% that means asset A moves opposite asset B that percent of the time.. From 1981 to 2010 gold moved in the same direction as Commodities 57% of the time – about half the time. That's fairly high correlation but 43% of the time gold doesn't move to same extent. It may move up or it may move down.

Look at Small Company Growth stocks. They move with the S&P500 index 83% of the time. That's huge. But, Small Company Value stocks only correlate 64%. That's why I don't use Small Growth stocks. They have too much correlation with something I already own.

Look at the various types of bonds. They move together closely. That's because when interest rates move, they all tend to move. It's very consistent. But look at Long Term Bonds and the S&P500. They correlate only 30%, which is low correlation. That's why advisors always suggest bonds should be in your portfolio. If stocks drop, the bonds likely won't drop. They could go up.

Gold is negatively correlated with bonds at -43%. This means the returns on bonds and gold tend to move opposite with moderate correlation. So, if you own gold, you should probably own some bonds too. If gold tanks, your bonds will move up and you won't lose as much. Later, we'll see how all the assets are best mixed. REITs pay a high dividend but are only 3% correlated with long term bonds and 40% correlated with the S&P500.

If you don't care for math like this, don't worry about it. I'm just laying the framework for how asset allocation works. Many people need proof before they'll accept an idea.

We're going to build a portfolio of different assets classes that takes advantage of weaker correlation and high returns. This way, if one goes down, another may go up. Over time, all assets go up, but at different times. Mixing the assets does not mean we'll get lower returns – not at all. Instead, the returns will be smoothed out. This is important: <u>Mixing the asset classes using correlation statistics means the entire portfolio won't be as volatile.</u> That's a good thing.

CORRELATION RISK

Most investors are not well served by a portfolio comprised of just large company stocks and some bonds. This is exactly what most investors get stuck with. They may own several stock funds, but because of manager changes and shifting strategies, there is no way to judge the correlation of such portfolios. Correlation analysis can only be done with index funds where manager style isn't an issue. Traditional portfolios may have high overall returns if stocks are really zooming, but they can go the other way just as easily during difficult times.

Clearly, if you're young and have a long time to invest, you can take on more correlation risk because things will average out over time. Older investors close to retirement or people finished working don't want that level of risk. That's because these investors can't afford to lose. Even young investors should avoid high correlation risk because they can get excellent returns with a more varied mix of assets.

Volatility refers to how much a portfolio jumps around in value. To not balance the assets in a portfolio means it is speculative. Speculative asset groupings will have big price swings. Technology looked good during the 1990's but lost 80% in 2001. Chasing commodities in 2006 led to disaster in 2008. Chasing hot stock market sectors, speculating in investments you know little about and trusting the luck of a celebrity fund manager are all different ways to take your portfolio off track and over a cliff.

CORRELATION COLLAPSE

Here is an important fact that is just as important as my explanation of statistical correlation.

Remember this: *During crashes and severe corrections in the stock market, the correlation between the asset classes breaks down. Investor panic causes all stock indexes to fall. Money rushes to cash and into short term fixed income investments.*

During a crash, the markets behave like a rack of billiard balls smacked by a high-speed cue ball. Assets scatter in various directions. What looks balanced and orderly during a calm market falls completely apart in tough times. The popular mutual funds can't protect assets because they're invested in only stocks and maybe some bonds. The funds' weightings of asset classes are a looming disaster for any person who can't afford to lose. This means retirees, the downsized and people in the late stages of their careers will likely suffer dire consequences when another crash or market disruption occurs.

The asset portfolios in this book are more protected from correlation breakdown because they hold asset mixes that offset each other. However, in a market crash even non-correlated assets won't completely protect you. It will certainly make a big difference but, for protection against crashes, you need market timing.

Many people today believe that bonds are immune to bad times. That is totally wrong thinking. Bonds can enter severe bear markets if interest rates rise rapidly during a credit crisis or war. You can lose money faster in a bond market crash than in any other asset class.

The absolute key thing to understand is we can construct a portfolio that will suffer less during a bond or stock market crash. Your stock and bond assets are better protected if properly allocated with offsetting asset classes.

The chart below shows the correlation of REITs, Commodity Futures, Gold, and Bonds relative to the S&P500 over thirty years and the percent losses when stocks crashed during 2001-2002 and 2008. The chart shows that during a crash asset correlation doesn't mean much. It's not predictable what will happen.

Asset Correlation with the S&P500 and Crash Loss %

	Correlation 1981-2010	Crash Year Losses 2001-2002	2008
REITs	40%	+21%	-37%
Commodities	38%	+.2%	-43%
Gold	-10%	+11%	+5%
Bonds	30%	+19%	+5%
S&P500		-34%	-37%

From 1981-2010 none of the other assets exhibited even moderate correlation with stocks. That's good because we wanted to avoid a high positive correlation with stocks during a crash. During the 2001-2002 crash, REITs, Commodities, Gold and Bonds all had positive returns. It proved the effectiveness of asset allocation to protect your money. That is usually true. In 2008 look what happened. REITS and Commodities lost more than stocks. Only gold and bonds went in the other direction.

From the above crash chart, now you can see that bonds are important to offset stocks. They move different from stocks during a crash. Money flees to the safety of fixed income. Gold also may benefit from a panic. But, stop right now! I'm warning you not to trust correlation statistics or history too much. Yes, the past can guide us. But, it is quite possible that, if long term interest rates skyrocketed during a credit panic, stocks could crash right along with bonds.

We don't know how assets will perform during the next crash. However, we can make a decision now to balance our assets with key objectives in mind.

TOM'S TIP:

Own some stocks regardless of your age
Include other assets that do well when stocks slump
Select asset classes with good historical returns
Use a simple market timing method to avoid steep losses

During the good years, stocks will perform very well and this is the normal condition. If you avoid stocks, your overall returns will be muted. Loading up only on bonds means your average returns will be low. If inflation rises, you could experience poor returns on bonds for a decade or more.

During bad years, our non-correlating assets will likely move in the opposite direction from stocks. During average years, most will move up but at different rates. If you can't afford to lose, then make correlation work to your advantage. This way, you get good long-term returns and better protection during a crash. During a prolonged bear market in stocks or bonds, your portfolio needs balanced assets to provide acceptable returns.

It's my belief that market timing can be used with a balanced portfolio to avoid devastating losses. It's not a guarantee but there's little risk to using it. I'll explain the technique later in this book.

12

BUILDING A SAFER PORTFOLIO

I'm going to present two portfolios that are a big improvement over a balanced mutual fund and a 60/40 standard allocation. To show results over a long period of time, I use the thirty years from 1981-2010. This is further broken down to show average returns over five, ten, and twenty year intervals. The number of losing years and largest loss give a good idea of how each portfolio will perform in the event of another market crash. The strategies I use take advantage of high returns and historical correlation to create a balanced portfolio. You'll probably get a feel for a strategy that suits you quickly. You'll no longer be flying blind.

As you review these portfolios, remember this. The future won't be like the past. From 1982-2010 we had an environment of falling interest rates, which was extremely positive for bonds. As interest rates fall, bonds do very well. You can't assume that a portfolio heavily weighted with bonds will do as well in the future. We're now in an environment of low long-term interest rates. This is usually positive for stocks, but we can't be sure how long it will last.

Even if you think stocks are too risky, I strongly advise you to choose a portfolio with some stocks in it – try 20-25%. Don't make the mistake of putting too much into long-term bonds. Bond investments are best mixed up with both short and long durations and offset with stocks. Again, balance is everything.

We have no way of knowing what range of returns to expect from any asset over the next couple decades. We can be fairly confident that the correlation, or lack thereof, between assets will continue to some extent like the past. Gold and bonds will likely continue to have negative correlation and the S&P500 and international stocks will have positive correlation. Even if things change somewhat, owning a broad range of assets will be to your benefit.

In the pages ahead, I'll use assets that have shown good long-term returns as I build the model portfolios. There are many ways to build a portfolio and I've geared mine towards the investor who can't afford to lose. I don't think my readers are interested in risk and volatility. You can easily change the percentages of the assets if you think I'm too conservative.

The next graphic lists the mutual fund and ETF symbols for the asset classes. It also shows the expense ratio and the benchmark index for the asset. For example, to invest money in the S&P500 index, you can use the fund VFINX or purchase the ETFs named SPY or VOO through your brokerage account. ETF and mutual fund products offered by other firms may also be acceptable. Remember, Wall Street's fund expenses, underperformance and an advisor fee will easily subtract at least 3% off your <u>annual</u> returns. I'm not exaggerating the impact of costs. Therefore, I'm using mostly low cost funds and ETFs offered by Vanguard.

Asset Classes	Fund Symbols & Expenses	
	Index Funds	ETF
International Stocks	VFWIX (.35)	VEU (.22)
S&P500	VFINX (.17)	SPY (.06)
Small Company Value	VISVX (.37)	VBR (.23)
US Aggregate Bonds	VBMFX (.22)	BND (.11)
Short Term Bond	VBISX (.22)	BSV (.11)
Money Market	VMFXX (.22)	N/A
Spot Gold	GTU, PHYS (.40)	GLD, IAU (.40)
REIT	VGSIX (.26)	VNQ (.12)
Commodity Futures	PCRIX (.74)	DBC (.81)

MUTUAL FUNDS AND ETF PRODUCTS TO USE

Mutual funds that track an index are good products for most investors. Most of the index products can be purchased through the Funds Network of many mutual fund companies with a low transaction fee.

Let's review some definitions again.

A funds network is simply a list of mutual funds offered by other companies that your fund company makes available to you. Mutual fund firms provide this service to their customers so people don't move all their cash to another firm. It's a good deal for the investor and all the companies involved.

A tracking index (or benchmark index) is a group of stocks based on size or investment style and a large provider of financial information tracks them daily. Thus Standard and Poors has the S&P500. Dow Jones, publisher of the Wall Street Journal, has the Dow Jones Industrial Average. There are many indexes for stocks and bonds, but the major ones cover broad sections of the markets.

Overseas investors often can't easily invest directly in US mutual funds but must use an ETF, Exchange Traded Fund, which tracks an index. For US investors, if your mutual fund company doesn't have a Funds Network then move your assets to Vanguard or another fund company that provides better services. If that isn't possible or practical, then open a brokerage account with your fund company and invest in an ETF product that tracks the index. The transaction fee to buy each ETF is reasonable – probably less than $35. Transfer money to the ETF once a year to keep transaction costs low.

There's a big difference between an index mutual fund and a managed mutual fund in the same asset class. The index fund eliminates fund manager biases, like second-guessing the market, over-weighting sectors and using dubious timing methods.

Using Other Mutual Funds

If a mutual fund company has a pure index fund that is benchmarked against the same index as the Vanguard fund and its expenses are low, then use it. You can find several low cost index funds that track the S&P500, but for the other asset classes, it may be difficult to find a good product. Be careful though with commodity funds.

My Thoughts on Commodities

I've decided not to use commodity futures in my portfolios for two reasons. First, petroleum makes up about half of the index. I believe investors should own gold. Considering the high correlation between gold and oil, a gold position already provides plenty of commodity exposure and in a physical form. The other reason is I'm uneasy with the ability of Wall Street to manipulate the futures markets. My concern may be misplaced but that's how I see it. I've included information on commodities for those who would like to own them.

There are several commodity index funds. The variants are not the same. They each allocate commodities differently because they track a different index. PCRIX tracks many commodities via the Dow Jones/AIG Commodity Index. DBC tracks the Deutsche Bank Liquid Commodity Index, which holds only six commodities. There are several other ETFs out there like RJI that track the Rogers commodities index. The commodity investing area is fairly new and things may standardize more in the future.

In the commodities area, it's important to understand the big distinction between a commodity and a company in the commodity business. Owning a natural resource mutual fund or energy fund that holds the stocks of various companies in the commodity business is not the same as owning PCRIX/DBC. The commodity index fund invests in "contract futures". In other words, they own a contract giving them the right to buy a physical commodity in the future at a specified price. Futures contracts are susceptible to discounts or premiums to the spot commodity price but it's all we have to track this sector. You can make good money on a commodity index by trading it with market timing.

BALANCED PORTFOLIOS

Lower portfolio risk is achieved by replacing some of the S&P500 index with REITs and by using Small Cap Value stocks. These assets have lower correlation with big company stocks and good returns by themselves. Then, a better mix of bonds is added to further balance it out. I use an aggregate bond fund rather than one with volatile long duration bonds. Aggregate bonds include issues of all durations. My portfolios are for passive investors who want something that works. These are people who simply can't take the risk of losing money. Maybe the investor is older. Perhaps it's a younger person frozen into inaction due to fear or uncertainty. Don't be ashamed if fear or emotional trauma has you super cautious. Remember, it's ok to be fearful.

Year after year, these portfolios offered better stability regardless of whether stocks were up or down. At some points during the year they might have been down a little, but by year-end they usually came back. They had some losing years, but they haven't lost heavily like an unbalanced portfolio.

If you can't afford to lose, then play it safe and sacrifice a small amount of annual return. You'll get much less risk and volatility. In addition, you'll probably win every year. This is how the smartest money in the world invests. Risk will always be increased if you increase and concentrate cash in a single stock class. That also holds for commodities and REITs. It's a mistake to concentrate your wealth in an asset just because it's performed well in the past. The past doesn't predict the future. My portfolios outperform the majority of managed stock and bond mixes most investors hold. The returns are fantastic when you consider that my portfolios hold less stock, bounce around less and rarely lose money. They have balance, low fees and let you ignore the Wall Street greed machine.

All financial markets have an upward bias. That's evident over time. Be aware that the upward tendency may go negative over part of your life.

Here's a summary of my portfolios compared to the 60/40 mix. When you consider the lower percentage of stocks and less losing years, on a risk adjusted basis my portfolios are attractive to an investor who can't afford to lose.

	60/40 Mix	Balanced #1	Balanced #2
5 years	5.3%	6.5%	6.1%
10 years	4.5%	7.3%	6.8%
20 years	9.4%	9.4%	8.6%
30 years	11.0%	11.0%	10.1%
Best Year	30.0%	27.9%	24.2%
Worst Year	-20.2%	-17.8%	-11.5%
Losing Years	6	3	1

The Balanced #1 portfolio holds 45% in stocks 45% in bonds and 10% in REITS. The stock positions are equally divided among international, S&P500 and Small Cap Value. The bond portion is 30% in the aggregate bond index and 15% in short term bonds. The portfolio matched the returns of the traditional 60/40 stock/bond mix for 20 and 30 years and routed it for the 5 and 10 year periods.

Balanced #1	%	Risk Level	
International Stocks	15	Best Year	27.9
S&P500	15	Worst Year	-17.8
Small Company Value	15	Losing Years	3
US Aggregate Bond	30	**Average Yearly Return %**	
Short Term Bond	15	5	6.5
REIT	10	10	7.3
		20	9.4
		30	11.0

My Balanced #2 portfolio has only 30% in stocks. It holds 60% in bonds but half of that is in super-safe short term bonds. It beat the 60/40 mix over 5 and 10 years and was quite close at 20 and 30 years.

Balanced #2	%	Risk Level	
International Stocks	10	Best Year	24.2
S&P500	10	Worst Year	-11.5
Small Company Value	10	Losing Years	1
US Aggregate Bond	30	**Average Yearly Return %**	
Short Term Bond	30	5	6.1
REIT	10	10	6.8
		20	8.6
		30	10.1

Don't forget, with my portfolios you aren't paying a financial advisor or any high mutual fund expenses. You aren't paying any front or back-end load fees. You actually receive the returns shown. If you use a financial advisor and managed funds, the 60/40 mix returns need to be reduced by 2-3% for the fees you pay each year! So, the 4.5% average return over 10 years would really be 2.5%. That's a huge hit to your portfolio. Now can you see why you can't seem to ever make money investing in the financial markets? The fees are killing you.

THE EFFECT OF FEES ON LIFETIME RETURNS

Let's be generous and assume that advisor fees and fund expenses only reduce your returns by 1.5% each year. The next chart shows how the growth of $10,000 in a 60/40 mix portfolio is reduced over 30 and 20 years.

Growth of $10,000	30 Years	20 Years
60/40 Mix	$191,800	$132,600
60/40 Mix - 1.5% fees	$126,900	$101,600
Balanced #1	$202,200	$105,800
Balanced #2	$169,200	$89,900

The 20 year cumulative growth of $10,000 tells us a lot. The 20 year period is from 1981 to 2000 and was a boom period for stocks and bonds. It was the highest returning 20 year period for both asset classes in US history. The 60/40 mix beat my Balanced portfolios growing to $132,000. After real-world expenses that drops by 30% to $101,000. My Balanced #1 portfolio earned $105,800 and my Balanced #2 earned $89,900. But, look what happens in the 30 year column which includes the market crash decade of 2001 to 2010. The 60/40 mix after expenses gains only 25% in that decade growing from $101,600 to $126,900. It barely matches inflation. My Balanced #1 almost doubles from $105,800 to $202,000 and my Balanced #2 grows 88% from $89,900 to $169,000. My portfolios accomplished this holding less stock and with less overall risk.

This chart shows the huge difference in asset growth from both avoiding high expenses and protecting your money better from the ravages of stock market crashes. My portfolios using passive investing with index funds will near guarantee a secure financial future.

PENSION FUND PERFORMANCE COMPARED TO MY PORTFOLIOS

Pension funds are managed for the beneficiaries and not to enrich Wall Street. They pay low fees and don't churn the capital to benefit the financial advisors. The secret to better portfolio performance is a balanced asset mix and low expenses. A simple mechanical approach to investing will do better than 97% of mutual funds and match the best pension funds. The chart below compares my portfolios to the annual percentage returns of two excellent pension funds.

Years	California CalPERS	Arizona ASRS	Balanced #1	Balanced #2
1986	24.6	32.1	21.8	18.8
1987	13.8	31.5	6.1	5.6
1988	3.9	11.8	15.8	13.1
1989	15.7	3.1	15.5	14.4
1990	9.7	14.3	-2.0	1.8
1991	6.5	9.5	20.6	18.4
1992	12.5	8.0	8.2	8.0
1993	14.5	14.6	15.2	12.9
1994	2.0	1.9	0.6	0.3
1995	16.3	17.8	20.5	18.7
1996	15.3	16.7	12.9	11.0
1997	20.1	20.6	15.9	13.6
1998	19.5	21.3	8.3	7.3
1999	12.5	16.8	6.4	4.4
2000	10.5	10.0	7.3	8.7
2001	-7.2	-6.7	2.5	4.8
2002	-5.9	-8.2	-2.9	0.5
2003	3.9	2.4	22.6	17.4
2004	16.7	17.5	12.7	10.2
2005	12.7	8.5	6.1	4.9
2006	12.3	9.8	15.2	12.4
2007	10.2	17.8	2.5	3.3
2008	-27.8	-7.6	-17.8	-11.5
2009	12.1	-18.1	19.4	15.4
2010	12.6	14.9	13.0	11.0
Avg	9.5	10.4	9.8	9.0

For the 25 year period my portfolios are highly competitive with the best pension funds in America. This proves that you can manage your own money and do as well as the pros. They get low expenses and so do you. You get returns just as good and hold a portfolio with even less risk. The pension funds hold about 10% of their assets in real estate and so do I. My portfolios hold less in stocks plus a balanced bond mix for a lower overall risk profile. Yes, you can do this at home!

It Gets Better

A balanced portfolio can reduce the sting of long market downturns by holding non-correlated asset classes in the right proportions. But, it can't eliminate all losses. Wouldn't it be great if you had a way to never lose during a market crash? Can you imagine how much your $10,000 would grow if you never had a losing year and were able to avoid prolonged downturns in the market? What I'm going to show you next will reduce the years you need to work and provide portfolio returns far beyond what you thought possible.

PART TWO

"The best kept secret in the investing world:
Almost nothing turns out as expected."

- Harry Browne

13

Introduction to Market Timing

Introduction to Market Timing

The prior chapters have explained asset correlation and how it can reduce portfolio volatility and overall risk. It can improve returns over the standard 60/40 stock/bond allocation. It reduces the number of losing years and smoothes out yearly returns. This alone is quite important for investors who can't afford to lose because they are less likely to panic out of their portfolio. For many people, proper asset allocation will be sufficient to grow and protect their wealth. The rest of this book will discuss market timing. This is for investors willing to take on some money management and learn ways to elevate their annual returns.

In the 60s and 70s the US stock market performed poorly because of inflation. After 1980, America issued debt to jumpstart economic growth. We borrowed and spent for thirty years to keep the economy expanding. That game is winding down in America as growth shifts to emerging markets.

The US has an enormous $14.5 trillion dollar federal debt and trillion dollar annual deficits. High and rising oil prices are inflationary and will be a drag on economic growth. I can't predict the future but I suspect we're entering an extended period of low growth, high unemployment and higher inflation.

What worked in the past may not work as well in the future. Investors need to be concerned about getting a return above the rate of inflation. Matching the S&P500 index may not be enough to grow your capital and maintain an acceptable standard of living. Some desperate investors will take on undue risk and incur large losses.

My advice is to pay attention to your portfolio returns and be prepared to adopt a new strategy. Market Timing can provide good returns in normal markets. Volatile markets are even better. I've worked on market timing models for years and have developed several sophisticated and some simple timing methods that produce impressive results. During the decade of the 2001-2010 market crashes, my personal portfolio more than doubled in value. The worst investing climate in modern history provided wonderful opportunities to sell at high points and buy back much lower.

The timing methods I'm presenting in this book are the moving average type. A moving average (MA) is the price today divided by the average price over a past period. So, if the S&P500 today is 1200 and the average price over the last year is 1150, that means today's price is above its 12 month moving average. The closing prices for the S&P500 index can be found on numerous financial websites, the evening news and in newspapers. (A good website is finance.yahoo.com)

Stated succinctly, moving average timing systems are effective at growing capital. They are easy to use and they work. Some other methods are better but moving averages will do the job. The big problem with a moving average market timing system is knowing what type of average to use. In other words, what is the correct cycle for the asset class? And, should we use daily, weekly or monthly data and a six month or twelve month moving average? I've written a computer program to test the moving average cycles for various asset classes. As you'll see in the following chapters, they're not the same for all.

MOVING AVERAGE MARKET TIMING RULE

Buy Signal: If the price is above the MA, stay in the market
Sell Signal: If the price falls below the MA, get out of the market

There's nothing complicated about a moving average but there are some things you need to understand.

1) A MA timing system will always buy and sell late. That means it won't buy at the absolute bottom of a market cycle or sell at the top. It will always buy and sell with a delay.

2) The key is to determine the cycle for a particular index that produces the optimum balance of infrequent trades and good gains.

3) A MA system only works with a broad asset class and you <u>must</u> use an index. It certainly works with the S&P500 stock index. It will not work with individual stocks or narrow market sectors like technology or small country indexes. That's because the price fluctuations are too great. Day trading with moving averages is a guaranteed way to lose money.

4) The objective isn't to beat buy and hold of an index over a long time. The objective is to make money on each trade and reduce risk by avoiding large draw downs of our capital.

My research shows that using monthly data is ideal. Broad markets like the S&P500 don't fluctuate that much over thirty days. Daily and weekly data create too many trades and performance is not significantly improved.

MY REQUIREMENTS FOR AN ACCEPTABLE MARKET TIMING SYSTEM

My investing temperament is probably like most readers of this book. I don't like risk and I don't like to lose money. The focus of this book is on safe investing. That doesn't mean beating the index at every point in time. It means avoiding steep downturns and crashes and taking advantage of superb buying opportunities. It means being able to cash out at any time and know I've done well. A successful moving average timing system should meet five requirements.

1. It must offer protection from extended bear markets.

2. It must be simple to use. Checking the market once a month is plenty.

3. It must have few trades. I know my readers aren't interested in becoming day traders or speculators.

4. It must deliver a high winning trade percentage.

5. It must have small losing trades. They must average under a 5% loss. Investors who can't afford to lose will not be philosophical about an average losing trade of 10%.

Bear markets often start with a sharp drop followed by a sideways market or a slight uptrend. Then, a longer decline ensues. Bull markets often begin with a choppy and nervous rising price trend. Trust the timing model at these turning points and wait for it to confirm the trend. The historical results you're about to see show convincingly that market timing the asset classes and moving to cash during danger periods is far superior to doing nothing. It might not sell or buy as early as you'd like but, in hindsight, it will have detected the new rising trend and protected most of your money from a decline.

SELECTING MARKETS FOR INVESTMENT

My research shows that less diversified global stock markets and high volatility indexes can't use the same moving average system as the S&P500 index. They require more time for the trend to become clear. Capital moves gradually into rising markets based on factors like corporate profits and price action. Once investors see the new trend, larger volumes of cash follow. The investors who buy in early make the most money but also incur the greatest risk. The conservative investor using my timing models will wait a few months for the trend to become established. This strategy will provide a large share of the gains while limiting the downside. In a weakening market, the timing model must get out before the crowd to avoid a sharp drop.

In this book I show the growth of capital over several decades comparing a moving average timing model to buy and hold of the same index. The real-world investor has a shorter investment horizon. For that reason, investors should focus more on making successful trades than on the historical rate of return. With my timing methods, you can trade a particular index or a world of markets. You can use the methods alongside other decision making criteria or to confirm trends you see developing. I suggest that readers consider investing in various global indexes as opportunity appears. The globalization trend is well established and the ETF products are available. Market timing combined with a global perspective may be the best way to succeed in the years ahead.

14

MARKET TIMING THE S&P500

FINDING THE BEST MOVING AVERAGE CYCLE

The calculations below use the S&P500 index without dividends. Thus my totals understate the performance of the timing model if it was compared to managed mutual funds over the same time periods. The average money market interest rate from 1952 to 2010 was 4.8%. I assume my moving average models earned a 4% annual rate when not in the stock market.

The "best" moving average system for a particular index is usually a range of moving averages depending on the time period. Let's look at the S&P500 over the sixty years from 1952 to 2010. The chart below shows a 12 month moving average produced the best gains beating buy and hold by 2.4 times. But, the highest percentage of winning trades was the 14 month moving average with a 79% trade success rate and 28 trades.

S&P500: 1952 to 2010				
MA Cycle	10	12	14	16
B&H	562,062	532,725	527,697	538,977
Model	1,082,193	1,310,572	1,053,391	1,204,694
%Better	1.93	2.46	2.00	2.24
Trades	43	33	28	27
%Success	0.65	0.70	0.79	0.81
Med Gain	14.67	17.69	19.69	15.63
Med Loss	-4.66	-4.38	-4.18	-3.80
Risk	0.68	0.70	0.71	0.71

Let's define the terms used.

B&H: Buy and Hold. This is total return on $10,000 invested and never sold for the time period.

Model: Returns on our market timing system using the number of months in our moving average timing cycle at the top of each column. This includes the interest earned while we were out of the market and in cash.

%Better: How the model compared to Buy and Hold. A number above 1 means it beat Buy and Hold.

Trades: This is the number of buy/sell transactions over the time period.

% Success: The percentage of trades that made money

Med Gain: This is the median gain of winning trades

Med Loss: The median loss of losing trades

Risk: The amount of time the model was invested in the market. .70 means 70%.

For the S&P500, moving average cycles of 10 to 16 months were the best performers. Cycles above and below that range symmetrically decreased in successful trades and profit. Few professional mutual fund managers ever beat the index over five years. Market timing did it for five decades.

Any of the cycles between 12 and 16 are acceptable. Within our acceptable group of MA cycles, a shorter MA cycle generally means more trades but higher gains. A longer cycle means less trades and usually lower gains. So, do you prefer a higher rate of return or less losing trades? Both the 12 and 14 month cycles are winners and you only have to make a trade once every two years on average. In the previous chart, the 12 month MA winning trades earned 17.6% on average and the losing trades averaged a minus 4.3%. That's a good win/loss rate. The 14 month MA earned 19.6% per winning trade and lost 4.1%. Both models were in the market only 70% of the time.

But, if we break it down into two thirty year periods, we get a slightly different story. First let's look at the 1952 to 1982 time period below. Again, the 12 month MA produced the best gains beating the index by 49% (1.49). Again, the 14 month MA had the best winning trades with 75% successful and only 16 trades.

S&P500: 1952 to 1982				
MA Cycle	10	12	14	16
B&H	48,626	48,528	46,165	46,165
Model	68,668	72,414	66,750	65,266
%Better	1.41	1.49	1.45	1.41
Trades	23	19	16	16
%Success	0.57	0.68	0.75	0.75
Med Gain	11.78	9.24	12.27	12.27
Med Loss	-4.58	-4.18	-3.80	-3.80
Risk	0.64	0.66	0.67	0.67

Now let's look at 1982 to 2010. The best cycle for winning trades was the 16 month MA with an incredible 90% success rate. It also had the best growth of $10,000 beating the index by 56% and only 10 trades.

S&P500: 1982 to 2010				
MA Cycle	10	12	14	16
B&H	107,606	107,606	107,606	106,792
Model	135,305	165,667	145,827	166,460
%Better	1.26	1.54	1.36	1.56
Trades	18	13	11	10
%Success	0.72	0.69	0.82	0.90
Med Gain	18.46	30.10	29.61	29.61
Med Loss	-6.14	-4.38	-4.58	-1.00
Risk	0.73	0.76	0.76	0.76

Since we can't predict the future, I'll pick the MA cycle in the middle. I think the 14 month MA is a good model for investors who can't afford to lose. It doesn't make the most money but it has about an 80% winning trade percentage and less overall trades. Let's make one more check. Let's investigate the boom and bust period from 1996 to 2010. Below is a chart of the S&P500 with the 14 month moving average in a dashed line.

The trade history at the end of this chapter shows there were five trades over these 15 years. 100% were winners which was above the historical average. Look how the 14 month MA bought the index in early 2003 right near the bottom of the bear market as the price went above the moving average. It sold again in late 2008 just below the peak as the price fell below the moving average. It bought again in mid 2009 but well above the market cycle bottom of 666. You'll notice that the buy and sell points are always later than the actual tops and bottoms. A $10,000 investment made in 1996 grew to $19,900 by late 2010 using buy and hold. The 14 month MA model grew that money to $36,000.

Shortcomings of MA Systems

The historical results are impressive but look closely at the January 1995 trade in the trade history list. The model sold in August 1998 at 957. The market continued upward. We had to buy back at October 1998 at 1098. That was 15% higher than our exit point. Buy and hold actually won that trade by not selling. This should be considered a trade failure but I only count actual losses not lost opportunity. This sort of event is called a whipsaw and is unavoidable with a moving average system. In 1998, after that experience, you would have doubted the value of this market timing system; that is until November of 2000 when you sold at 1315 and avoided a 36% drop to 963.

A moving average system always buys and sells with a delay. None were able to avoid the 1987 stock market crash. The 14 month MA model bought in August of 1984 at 166. The S&P500 ran up to 330 by August of 1987. The model sold in October of 1987 at 252. Yes, the 1984 trade earned 17% per year even after the crash but people hate seeing their portfolio fall from a recent peak.

I remember the 1987 crash. The 30% drop from the peak was nerve wracking. If you want to use a MA timing system then accept the occasional disappointments. Over your investing lifetime it will more than make up for the infrequent losses and missed opportunities. Here's a tip. If you see the market dipping and are concerned, switch to checking the weekly closing price on Friday. If the market is drifting below its 14 month MA for a couple weeks, you could sell early if you don't think it can't recover by month end. That's called using judgment. Another way to get perspective is to follow the advanced market timing alerts on my website at www.gleasonreport.com.

The 14 Month MA System

From the research results, I think we can safely say that the 14 month MA is good enough to use because it stood the test of a bull market and a ferocious bear market decade. It actually grew your capital impressively. A 12 month system is also fine.

We don't know what returns the stock market will provide in the future but this is the kind of market beating performance you can reasonably expect. I hope I've convinced you of the incredible power of market timing. Even a person on a modest income with little saving ability can earn a tremendous pot of money or avoid losing it. If a one-time investment earns this much, just imagine what saving and investing a few thousand more each year into a Roth IRA would accomplish.

Timing Rule for the S&P500

Buy Rule: If the month end price is greater than the 14 month MA then buy.

Sell Rule: If the month end price is less than the 14 month MA then sell.

How to Calculate the 14 Month Moving Average

Record the closing price of the S&P500 on the last trading day of each month. (You can actually use any day of the month. Just be consistent). At the end of each monthly period, add up the 14 months and divide by 14. If the S&P500 is above that number stay in the market. If it's below, sell.

Apr-10	1206
May-10	1089
Jun-10	1090
Jul-10	1101
Aug-10	1064
Sep-10	1148
Oct-10	1183
Nov-10	1180
Dec-10	1257
Jan-11	1286
Feb-11	1322
Mar-11	1325
Apr-11	1363
May-11	1345
Average	**1211**

The S&P500 on May 31, 2011 is at 1345 and above the 14 month MA of 1211. We stay in the stock market.

S&P500 14 MONTH MA TRADE HISTORY 1952 TO 2010

Here are the trade dates for the 14MA system. My objective here is to compare buy and hold to the timing model. For ease of calculation, I start buy and hold on the same month as when the model does its first trade. Both trades are closed on 12/31/2010. Remember, the results do not include reinvested dividends but I have included interest at 4%.

Action	Date	Price	Model	B&H
BUY	Mar-53	25.3	10,000	
SELL	Apr-53	24.6	9,735	9,735
In Cash			292	
BUY	Jan-54	26.1	10,027	
SELL	Sep-56	45.4	17,436	17,931
In Cash			174	
BUY	Dec-56	46.7	17,610	
SELL	Jan-57	44.7	16,875	17,682
In Cash			225	
BUY	May-57	47.4	17,100	
SELL	Aug-57	45.2	16,303	17,880
In Cash			489	
BUY	May-58	44.1	16,792	
SELL	Jan-60	55.6	21,179	21,988
In Cash			777	
BUY	Dec-60	58.1	21,956	
SELL	Apr-62	65.2	24,650	25,796
In Cash			739	
BUY	Jan-63	66.2	25,389	
SELL	Jun-65	84.1	32,262	33,262
In Cash			108	
BUY	Jul-65	85.3	32,370	
SELL	May-66	86.1	32,704	34,056
In Cash			872	

BUY	Jan-67	86.6	33,576	
SELL	Feb-68	89.4	34,642	35,334
In Cash			231	
BUY	Apr-68	97.5	34,873	
SELL	Feb-69	98.1	35,113	38,801
In Cash			117	
BUY	Mar-69	101.5	35,230	
SELL	Jun-69	97.7	33,911	38,635
In Cash			1,922	
BUY	Nov-70	87.2	35,832	
SELL	Oct-71	94.2	38,721	37,259
In Cash			258	
BUY	Dec-71	102.1	38,979	
SELL	Apr-73	107.0	40,843	42,297
In Cash			2,995	
BUY	Feb-75	81.6	43,838	
SELL	Feb-77	99.8	53,633	39,470
In Cash			2,503	
BUY	Apr-78	96.8	56,135	
SELL	Oct-78	93.2	54,002	36,832
In Cash			360	
BUY	Dec-78	96.1	54,362	
SELL	Mar-80	102.1	57,744	40,367
In Cash			192	
BUY	Apr-80	106.3	57,937	
SELL	Aug-81	122.8	66,931	48,552
In Cash			2,677	

BUY	Aug-82	119.5	69,608	
SELL	Feb-84	157.1	91,479	62,103
In Cash			1,830	
BUY	Aug-84	166.7	93,308	
SELL	Oct-87	251.8	140,954	99,561
In Cash			5,168	
BUY	Sep-88	271.9	146,122	
SELL	Apr-90	330.8	177,769	130,802
In Cash			593	
BUY	May-90	361.2	178,361	
SELL	Aug-90	322.6	159,268	127,544
In Cash			2,654	
BUY	Jan-91	343.9	161,922	
SELL	Mar-94	445.8	209,868	176,263
In Cash			3,498	
BUY	Aug-94	475.5	213,366	
SELL	Nov-94	453.7	203,584	179,395
In Cash			1,357	
BUY	Jan-95	470.4	204,941	
SELL	Aug-98	957.3	417,044	378,521
In Cash			2,780	
BUY	Oct-98	1098.7	419,825	
SELL	Nov-00	1315.0	502,470	519,948
In Cash			50,247	
BUY	May-03	963.6	552,717	
SELL	Jan-08	1378.6	790,738	545,096
In Cash			47,444	

BUY	Jul-09	987.5	838,183	
SELL	Aug-10	1064.0	903,134	420,719
In Cash			3,010	
BUY	9/10/2010	1148.0	906,144	
SELL	1/1/2011	1286.0	1,015,071	508,501

15

TIMING THE GOLD MARKET

GOLD IS REAL MONEY

I believe investors should hold a sizeable percentage of their money in gold at all times. I call this Core Gold. Ideally, it should be held as physical bullion in your personal possession. Others will say that 5% in gold is enough. I think that's too little. Gold should not be considered a portfolio asset. If you chose to own some gold then consider it a form of safety insurance and don't think of it as a financial investment that will earn an expected return. Buy gold coins regularly and don't tell others about it.

I worked as a bullion dealer for some years and understand the emotional lure of this fabulous metal. It is the world's truest form of real money and has remarkable beauty. Gold is in a class by itself. It's valuable to own when nations are in severe political turmoil or during a financial breakdown.

Physical gold doesn't show up on a bank statement. It's invisible. Greedy and litigious people can hire all the lawyers they want but good luck finding it. They can't steal what they can't see. Gold is easily transported and is accepted everywhere in the world for the same price. It's your ace in the hole against disaster, betrayal and litigation. Never sell unless you must start over, escape or you face a dire emergency. Emergency doesn't mean you want to start a business, buy a new car or get braces for your kid.

Gold rose in the 1970s along with oil prices. In 1971 America went off the gold standard and in 1973 America worked a deal with the Saudis so oil was only priced in dollars. In effect, we then went on the oil standard. This arrangement protected the Saudi royal family and the dollar. Gold usually has positive correlation with oil prices.

Gold/Oil Correlation

1970s.......97%
1980s........ 4%
1990s.......29%
2000s.......82%

People are afraid of gold today because it performed so poorly from 1982 to 2001 and had twelve losing years. Gold was above $600 in 1980 and would fall to the $250 range in 2001. Why did that happen and why was the positive correlation much lower in the 80s and 90s?

By 1980 gold had been speculated up in price due to the rampant inflation of the 70s.. During the early 80s large supplies of new oil were discovered in Alaska, Russia and in the North Sea. In addition, advances in technology and drilling recovered more oil from existing wells. Suddenly, oil was plentiful again. In addition, as inflation fell, interest rates became positive and gold became vulnerable. Oil prices dropped but gold declined at a much faster rate and the correlation between the two commodities broke down. Oil remained plentiful through the mid 1990s.

By 2000, it was clear that oil production worldwide was peaking. The world now struggles to find new oil. The gold/oil correlation zoomed up after 2000. Gold rose as oil rose.

We are in the age of Peak Oil. Geologists use this term to describe a point where production from existing wells goes into decline and new oil discoveries can't replace the losses. Essentially, this means the point where petroleum prices will rise relentlessly. Production rates are falling across the globe pressuring the world economy and paper currencies. America has already started wars to lock up oil resources. China is buying up oil and commodities across the globe. This is a sure sign of energy and military troubles ahead. As oil rises, gold will rise too.

How to Own Gold

There are two right ways an investor can own physical Core Gold. You can buy physical gold coins or own a fund that holds the physical, allocated metal. For physical gold, the popular coins minted by governments are excellent: US Eagle or Buffalo, Canadian Maple Leaf, South African Krugerrand, Austrian Philharmonic, etc. Buy coins that are one ounce or fractions of an ounce. Don't buy commemorative coins from private mints or collector coins. The markups are huge and the collectible value is dubious.

A variety of gold funds are now available. Some are appropriate for speculation and others for owning gold in a retirement account. For example, the Central Gold Trust (GTU) and Sprott Physical Gold Trust (PHYS) are Canadian closed-end mutual funds that own the actual metal and store it in vaults. They retain title and never loan it out. This is called "allocated" gold. That means it's not mixed with someone else's gold. Funds with 100% allocated gold are good choices for a retirement account.

ETF products like GLD and IAU are tracking indexes. These funds don't hold all allocated gold and are fine for speculative trading.

GTU and PHYS are Closed End Funds. That means their shares will sell at a premium or discount to the gold price until they increase or dispose of some of their gold. Their advantage is that profits are taxed at the capital gains rate in a taxable account rather than at the full tax rate of gold coins and the tracking indexes.

Mining stocks are not the same thing as bullion – not even close. Mining stocks are companies in the business of commodity exploration. A company like Barrick Gold (ABX) mines for gold. Most mining firms are speculative enterprises and are prone to booms and busts. This usually has less to do with the price of gold and is more about what mines they own and the costs of extracting the metal. Gold prices and mining shares do not move in tandem.

Market timing is valuable when buying or selling gold. I've discovered several ways to time the gold market with a high success rate. Negative interest rate environments are the best years to hold gold. When the rate of inflation exceeds the interest rate on a safe money market account, investors are being robbed by the government. This is indeed positive for gold because money flees the currency. There's a problem though with the negative interest rate method.

Governments can lie about their inflation rate or manipulate interest rates. Real interest rates then become hard to calculate. In 2011 the American government is holding down short rates and using statistical manipulations to hide inflation from the public. This should be a red warning flag that there is big trouble ahead. The enormous federal deficits will require cuts to defense spending and Medicare. Rather than make a frontal assault on entitlement spending, they'll likely do means testing. They'll reduce real benefits by inflating away debt and understating the Consumer Price Index (CPI).

HOW TO ESTIMATE A FAIR GOLD PRICE

A research paper I authored (The Real Gold Standard) showed that gold has historically sold at an average of 16 times the price of oil. The standard deviation of that average is too wide for it to be a good way to time gold. It does though give us an idea of what the fair value price of gold should be. If the 12 month moving average of oil is $100 and gold is $1400, that roughly indicates gold is under priced by $200/oz (16 x 100 = $1600). I'd be a buyer of gold since I know oil will rise for the rest of my life.

Governments can intervene in markets but they can't fake prices for long because they're up against shrewd people who won't participate in a rigged game. I use moving averages in this book because price action is hard to fake and I need to present a simple method you can use.

TIMING GOLD PURCHASES AND SALES

Gold is a volatile asset class; more so than the stock market. A moving average timing system must be tweaked a bit to smooth out gold's jumpy price action. With gold we can't use a one month change to signal a new direction. We need more confirmation via a series of steps in the new direction. We want to see three months of a rising moving average before we buy. We want two months of a falling moving average before we sell. Markets usually fall much faster than they rise so we can't linger long on the sell side.

THE 3/2 STEP METHOD FOR GOLD TIMING

Buy Rule: If the month end price is greater than the 12 month MA for three consecutive months, then buy.

Sell Rule: If the month end price is less than the 12 month MA for two consecutive months, then sell.

Here's the moving average history for gold since 1974 using various cycles and the 3/2 Step Method. (Prices prior to that are useless since gold bullion was illegal to own in America). This chart shows the growth of a $10,000 investment made in 1974. (Refer to the S&P500 chapter for an explanation of the bold titles in the far left column).

Gold 1974 through 2010				
MA Cycle	8	10	12	14
B&H	77,562	86,808	86,416	83,970
Model	147,046	211,955	230,665	192,910
%Better	1.90	2.44	2.67	2.30
Trades	15	13	11	11
%Success	0.53	0.54	0.64	0.55
Med Gain	39.32	44.44	36.14	50.08
Med Loss	-4.82	-2.78	-3.04	-2.78
Risk	0.53	0.55	0.55	0.54

Market timing greatly outperforms the buy and hold of gold. Also, the model gains above do not include any accumulated interest earned when out of the gold market. (With 4% interest, the timing model would grow $10,000 to $500,000 and beat buy and hold by 5 times).

The 12 month MA is the best in my opinion and beats buy and hold by 2.67 times. There were only 11 trades in near forty years. 64% of the trades are successful which isn't great but the median losing trade is small averaging only 3%. Winning trades averaged 36% gains.

Look at the median loss row in the chart above. I use the median average and not the arithmetic average for showing losses and gains. Median means the one in the middle. If there are three losing trades then the middle trade is the median. This is not the mathematical average loss of all three trades. That distinction is important because if you see a low median loss it can mask a huge larger loss. That's why viewing the actual trade history is important.

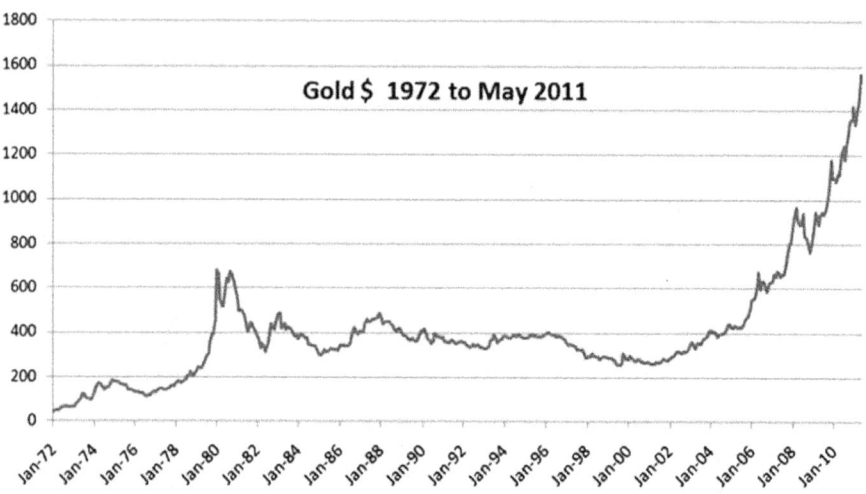

Gold $ 1972 to May 2011

Below are the trade dates from 1974 to 2010. The model was still in gold at January 2011 with gold at $1335. I forced the year-end sale to equally compare the model to buy and hold at the end of 2010.

The largest loss was 11% in 1990. The other losing trades were 1%, 4% and 3%. These occurred during the long gold bear market years of 1981 to 2000. The timing model didn't lose much and that's quite encouraging. This gold model is in the market only 57% percent of the time.

Also notice that the model did not sell gold in 1980 at the brief peak. It didn't sell until it had fallen to $499. That's because gold was at high levels only briefly and didn't pull up the average. This provides a lesson for using all moving average systems. Don't buy during the middle of a trade if the price has already risen rapidly. Get in early or don't buy again until a new cycle begins.

I should also mention that I did find a gold timing cycle that produced exceptional returns but the surrounding trades lacked the symmetry I require. A 4/3 step model with a 10 month moving average produced an 80% trade success rate and beat buy and hold by 2.3 times. It had ten trades. However, the 8 and 12 month MAs only had a 50% success rate. I mention this as both an opportunity for your investigation and as a warning. There are people who will grab that statistic and claim they have a better system than Gleason or use it to disparage my work. I'm aware of MAs that do better than the ones I recommend. Without symmetry, these might be aberrations but maybe not. Remember, this book is written for the investor who can't afford to lose.

If your core gold value grows too large relative to your desired allocation, then sell using the timing model Add to core gold regularly and buy aggressively when the timing model is positive. Don't be lured by a big profit and sell your core gold prematurely during a bull market. Trouble comes in many forms and you may need that gold stash when least expected.

Action	Date	Price	Model	B&H
BUY	Oct-74	159.0	10,000	
SELL	Jul-75	165.2	10,389	10,389
In Cash			0	
BUY	Jan-77	132.2	10,389	
SELL	Jan-81	555.8	43,682	34,961
In Cash			0	
BUY	Nov-82	415.2	43,682	
SELL	Jul-83	422.6	44,459	26,581
In Cash			0	
BUY	Oct-85	325.9	44,459	
SELL	Mar-88	443.6	60,525	27,903
In Cash			0	
BUY	Jan-90	410.5	60,525	
SELL	May-90	369.1	54,416	23,213
In Cash			0	
BUY	Jun-93	371.9	54,416	
SELL	Dec-94	379.3	55,489	23,855
In Cash			0	
BUY	Jun-95	387.6	55,489	
SELL	Sep-95	383.1	54,847	24,096
In Cash			0	
BUY	Jan-96	400.5	54,847	
SELL	Jul-96	383.6	52,531	24,126
In Cash			0	
BUY	Dec-99	283.1	52,531	
SELL	Aug-00	274.5	50,935	17,263
In Cash			0	
BUY	Oct-01	283.1	50,935	
SELL	Sep-08	829.9	149,340	52,201
In Cash			0	
BUY	Apr-09	889.5	149,340	
SELL	Jan-11	1335.0	224,137	83,970

How to Construct the 3/2 Step Moving Average Model

Record the month end price of gold. Each month add up current month plus the prior eleven months and divide by 12. This is the 12 month moving average. Divide the current month end price by the MA.

Buy Rule: If the month end price is greater than the 12 month MA for <u>three</u> consecutive months, then buy.

Sell Rule: If the month end price is less than the 12 month MA for <u>two</u> consecutive months, then sell.

Date	Gold	12mo MA
Nov-08	760.9	870.7
Dec-08	822.0	872.3
Jan-09	859.2	869.8
Feb-09	**943.2**	**871.5**
Mar-09	**924.3**	**867.8**
Apr-09	**889.5**	**866.1**
May-09	930.2	869.4
Jun-09	945.7	874.1
Jul-09	934.2	873.7
Aug-09	949.7	882.9
Sep-09	1007.0	897.7
Oct-09	1044.0	917.5

In the price history above, gold was above its 12 month MA in February, March and April of 2009. We buy gold at $889 on April 30, 2009. As of June 2011, gold is at $1500. The 3/2 Step Model for gold is also useful for timing the bond market as you'll see in the next chapter.

THE NEGATIVE INTEREST RATE GOLD MODEL

Previously, I discussed how gold does well when real interest rates are negative. A negative interest rate means the rate you receive on a safe money market fund is below the rate of inflation.

Money Market Rate minus Inflation Rate = Real Interest Rate

Gold rises when real rates are negative because the purchasing power of paper money is losing to inflation. We buy gold when real rates are negative and sell gold when real rates go above 2%. The market is hesitant to abandon gold until convinced real rates will remain positive. This model is excellent and rarely trades.

For pricing inflation, I'm using the official US Bureau of Labor Statistics CPI rate (http://www.bls.gov/schedule/archives/cpi_nr.htm#2009). For the money market rate, I'm using the Federal Reserve 3-month Treasury Constant Maturity Rate (http://research.stlouisfed.org/fred2/data/GS3M.txt).

Negative Interest Rate Gold Timing Rule

Buy gold when real interest rates are below zero
Sell gold when real interest rates are greater than 2%

It's fine to wait for a couple months of negative real rates before buying gold. Once real rates go above 2% or you see a gradual rising trend toward that number, sell gold. Don't linger too long because markets fall much faster than they rise.

	Date	Real Rate	Gold
Buy	Oct 70	-0.3	38
Sell	Jul 73	+2.3	120
Buy	Oct 73	-.06	100
Sell	Dec 80	+2.3	593
Buy	Oct 92	-0.3	345
Sell	Oct 94	+2.3	390
Buy	Sep 01	-0.1	283

The model is still in gold in May 2011 with gold at $1500. Real rates remain negative. $10,000 invested in October 1973 would have grown to $350,000 in 2011 without interest. The model was in the market only half of those 38 years.

16

TIMING THE BOND MARKET

You make the most money in bonds when interest rates are falling. That's because the older bonds have higher yields and pay more interest. Conversely, rising interest rates will reduce the profit from holding bonds because new bonds pay a higher yield than the old ones.

Rising rates can be extraordinarily dangerous for bond owners if the rates rise suddenly. If rates rise slowly then the bond interest may be larger than the decline in principal. Regardless, rising rates reduce your return.

Let's say you buy a 20 year corporate bond paying 5%. If, over one year, interest rates rise to 6.5% the value of your bond falls by 30%. You still get your 5% interest payment. Your $1000 bond can be redeemed for its full value in twenty years but can only be sold for $700 today. That's because newer bonds pay much more interest and prospective buyers will require a discounted price from you.

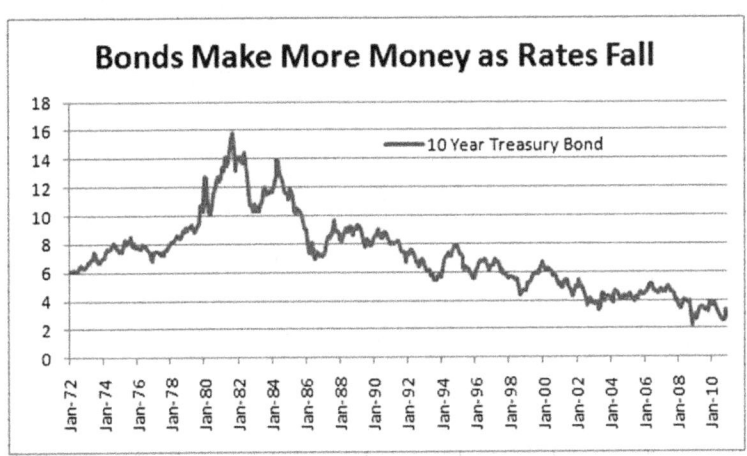

The inflationary 1970s were tough on bond owners. Rates sky-rocketed from 6% in 1972 to 15% in 1981. Investors received their 6% annual interest rate payment from their bond but inflation hit 9% in 1975 and 13% in 1980. Owning bonds was a loser. By 1981 few wanted to own a treasury bond. Then something happened. The government got inflation under control and interest rates fell for the next 30 years. The bond bull market was as profitable as the stock market for those years.

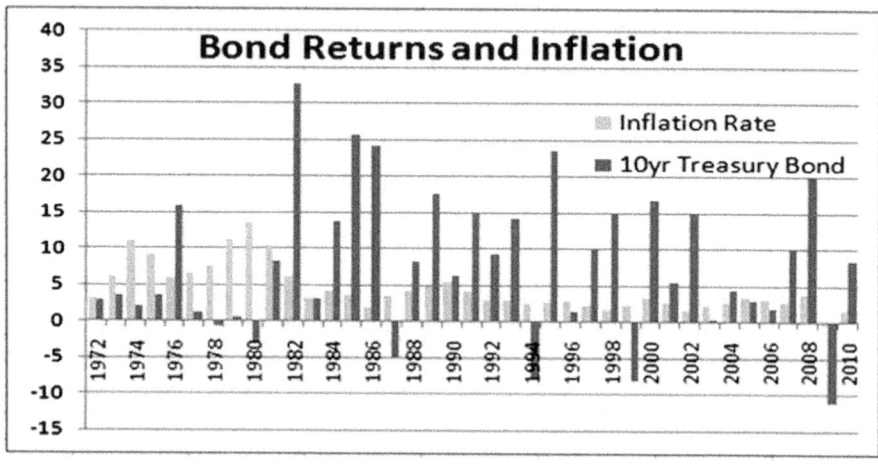

Bond market risk shocked investors in the 1970s because returns were low relative to inflation. Here in 2011, most people aren't aware of the danger that lurks with interest rates near record lows. The ten year treasury bond is under 3% in May 2011. The US government has over $14 trillion in debt and will never pay it off except through default or inflation. Do you really want to hold long term treasury bonds?

You can gather a steady stream of bond income simply by holding an aggregate bond fund with a shorter duration. Vanguard offers a Total Bond Market Income ETF called BND or its mutual fund equivalent VBMFX. It holds a sampled equivalent of every corporate and treasury bond. It only had two losing years in the last 25 and the largest loss was -2.6%.

The aggregate bond fund has a shorter duration and that reduces the risk profile. Rather than timing the bond market, most investors could hold BND/VBMFX or a similar fund or ETF and use it for the bond allocation of their portfolio. If you are certain interest rates will rise, then own a bond fund with a very short duration like VBISX. This fund will more closely track short term interest rates and will rise in value if inflation goes up.

It is possible to time the bond market but bonds are complicated. The investor who can't afford to lose should hold a bond index fund with a balanced mix of bonds. Some investors may want to take on more risk for more returns.

Earlier in the book I explained how bonds and gold are negatively correlated. Bond values tend to fall (rates go up) as gold rises. Bond values tend to rise (rates go down) when gold falls.

Bond Market Timing Method

Buy bonds when you exit gold.
Sell bonds when you buy gold.

The bond market is driven by the same factors as the gold market except in reverse. Fear causes gold to rise and confidence causes gold to fall. Therefore, to time the bond market, we simply switch between gold and bonds. You'll make more profit after a gold sale by switching to bonds rather than putting your cash into a money market fund. To further limit risk, buy a shorter duration bond fund. If you're a risk tolerant personality, then long duration bonds will provide bigger profits.

The table below shows the interest rate on the 10 year Treasury bond at the gold sell and buy dates. Thus the gold sell date is when we buy bonds. The gold buy date is when we sell bonds. Any moving average that works for gold will also work for bonds. I'm the first person (that I know of) to ever publish this simple and profitable timing model.

Observe, how in every instance, interest rates fall between the bond buy and sell dates. So, not only does the bond investor earn the interest, they also get a nice capital gain. Look at the Buy in September 1983. You would have bought the ten year bond with the yield at 11.4%. You earned that yearly rate until you sold the bond in December 1985. You earned 11.4% per year plus a 24% capital gain. If you were using a 20 year bond, the interest rate would be higher and the capital gain would be doubled.

Then in December 1985, when you sold the bond, you would have bought gold at $321 and sold it in March of 1988 at $443 earning a 38% gain. On and on. This shows how profitable the gold-bond swing trade can be. You could make a living just switching between these two asset classes.

It's true that interest rates trended lower from 1982 to 2010 but there were some big jumps up in rates along the way. I'll guarantee you that many investors panicked out of their bonds and took losses. It's also true that a buy and hold bond investor did well over those 30 years. But, we don't know what the future holds. The objective of market timing for the investor who can't afford to lose is to reduce risk. We need to make successful trades and steadily grow our portfolio.

Action	Date	Interest Rate	Capital Gain
Buy	Jul-75	8.2	
Sell	Jan-77	7.4	8%
Buy	Feb-81	13.4	
Sell	Nov-82	10.8	26%
Buy	Sep-83	11.4	
Sell	Dec-85	9.0	24%
Buy	Mar-88	8.6	
Sell	Jan-90	8.4	2%
Buy	May-90	8.6	
Sell	Jun-93	5.8	28%
Buy	Jan-95	7.6	
Sell	Jun-95	6.2	14%
Buy	Sep-95	6.2	
Sell	Jan-96	5.6	6%
Buy	Jul-96	6.8	
Sell	Dec-99	6.4	4%
Buy	May-00	6.3	
Sell	Oct-01	4.3	20%
Buy	Oct-08	4.0	
Sell	Apr-09	3.1	9%
Buy	Jan-11	3.4	

17

TIMING GLOBAL STOCK MARKETS

In this chapter I'll summarize my research on using moving average timing systems with world stock market indexes. To my knowledge, this information has never before been published.

Investors in major industrialized nations naturally want to use market timing with their home market. In addition, enterprising investors want the option of deploying capital around the world wherever opportunity may exist. I have good news. My market timing system works as well overseas as in the United States. Actually, it may work even better.

I have twenty-five years of data for some of these world markets and I think that is sufficient to have confidence in the timing system. For some emerging markets, I only have fifteen years. The same timing technique appears to work for most of them which indicates it may be a universal process for the more volatile indexes.

In all cases I'm using a Step Method with monthly data whereas in the US I used a simple 12 month moving average. The Step Method you'll recall was used to time the gold market. It also works well overseas. Few, if any, stock markets around the globe have the depth and breadth of America's S&P500. Unlike America, dominant corporations and industries in smaller nations tend to have more influence on the stock index. The Step Method smmoothes out the index. For all these foreign markets, the index price data does not include reinvested dividends. I used a 4% rate to calculate money market interest when out of the index. In Japan, I used 2% because rates were much lower there.

You can gather price information and view graphs for all these indexes at Yahoo Finance (http://finance.yahoo.com/intlindices?e=americas).

Let's review these markets starting with China's Hang Seng stock index.

The Hong Kong (China) Hang Seng Index

The Hang Seng Index (abbreviated: HSI) is used to record and monitor daily changes of the largest companies of the Hong Kong stock market. The 45 constituent companies represent about 60% of capitalization of the Hong Kong Stock Exchange.

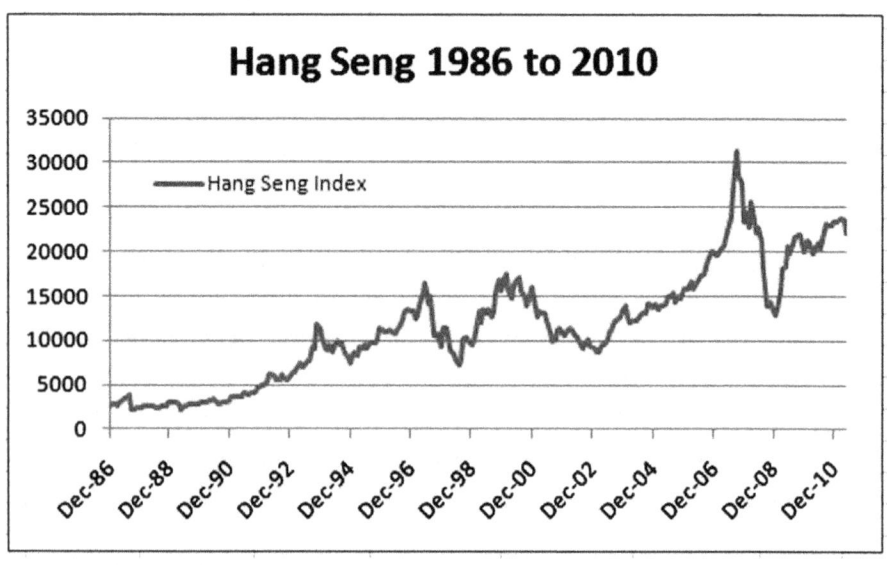

Hang Seng: 1988 to 2010				
MA Cycle	8	10	12	14
B&H	87,249	87,249	87,249	87,249
Model	64,323	95,504	109,458	104,882
%Better	0.74	1.09	1.25	1.20
Trades	13	10	8	7
%Success	0.69	0.80	0.75	0.71
Med Gain	31.27	31.27	48.23	39.17
Med Loss	-15.09	-2.16	-2.16	-2.16
Risk	0.61	0.61	0.65	0.69

Several timing cycles between eight and fourteen months successfully work with the Hang Seng. I've picked the 12 month MA. The success rate is acceptable and it beats buy and hold. There were two losses. The first one in 1988 lost 18%. The second lost 2%. The Hong Kong market has matured since 1988. I think we'll see a more western style price pattern going forward.

HANG SENG 3/2 STEP TIMING METHOD

Buy Rule: If the month end price is greater than the 12 month MA for <u>three</u> consecutive months, then buy.

Sell Rule: If the month end price is less than the 12 month MA for <u>two</u> consecutive months, then sell.

Action	Date	Price	Model	B&H
BUY	Dec-88	2687.4	10,000	
SELL	Jun-89	2273.9	8,461	8,461
In Cash			282	
BUY	Apr-90	2951.0	8,743	
SELL	Oct-90	2990.0	8,859	11,125
In Cash			148	
BUY	Mar-91	3745.0	9,007	
SELL	Oct-94	9646.3	23,199	35,894
In Cash			696	
BUY	Jul-95	9453.4	23,895	
SELL	Nov-97	10526.9	26,608	39,171
In Cash			1,153	
BUY	Dec-98	10048.6	27,761	
SELL	Oct-00	14895.3	41,152	55,426
In Cash			4,664	
BUY	Aug-03	10909.0	45,816	
SELL	Feb-08	24331.7	102,188	90,539
In Cash			5,791	
BUY	Jul-09	20573.3	107,979	
SELL	Jun-10	20129.0	105,647	74,901
In Cash			1,761	
BUY	Nov-10	23008.0	107,407	
SELL	Jan-11	23447.3	109,458	87,249

ENGLAND FTSE INDEX

The FTSE 100 Index or, informally, the 'footsie' is a share index of the 100 most highly capitalized UK companies listed on the London Stock Exchange.

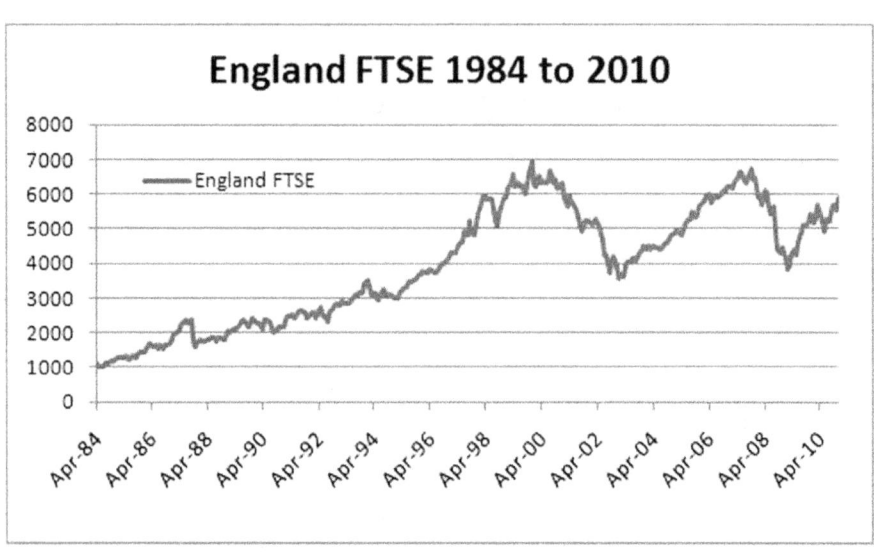

England FTSE 1984 to 2010

FTSE: 1985 to 2010				
MA Cycle	10	12	14	16
B&H	45,413	47,476	43,717	42,571
Model	49,540	44,267	48,526	40,753
%Better	1.09	0.93	1.11	0.96
Trades	10	9	8	8
%Success	0.80	0.78	0.88	0.75
Med Gain	12.47	14.20	14.20	16.22
Med Loss	-4.23	-3.48	-3.48	-3.48
Risk	0.61	0.65	0.67	0.69

Market timing works best with the 14 month MA. Our $10,000 initial investment beats buy and hold by 11%. It had only one small loss of 3.5%. It's in the market 67% of the time. There were only 8 round-trip trades over 25 years and 88% of the trades were successful.

I'd feel confident using market timing with the FTSE because of the high success rate across all the moving averages.

FTSE 3/2 STEP TIMING METHOD

Buy Rule: If the month end price is greater than the 12 month MA for <u>three</u> consecutive months, then buy.

Sell Rule: If the month end price is less than the 12 month MA for <u>two</u> consecutive months, then sell.

Action	Date	Price	Model	B&H
BUY	Aug-85	1341.1	10,000	
SELL	Nov-87	1579.9	11,781	11,780
In Cash			510	
BUY	Dec-88	1793.1	12,291	
SELL	Sep-90	1990.2	13,642	14,840
In Cash			318	
BUY	Apr-91	2486.2	13,960	
SELL	Jul-92	2399.6	13,474	17,892
In Cash			180	
BUY	Nov-92	2778.8	13,654	
SELL	Jun-94	2919.2	14,344	21,767
In Cash			526	
BUY	May-95	3319.4	14,870	
SELL	Sep-98	5064.4	22,687	37,763
In Cash			302	
BUY	Jan-99	5896.0	22,989	
SELL	Feb-00	6232.6	24,302	46,473
In Cash			3,483	
BUY	Sep-03	4091.3	27,785	
SELL	Feb-08	5884.3	39,961	43,876
In Cash			2,531	
BUY	Sep-09	5133.9	42,492	
SELL	Jan-11	5862.9	48,526	43,717

GERMANY DAX

The DAX is a blue chip stock market index consisting of the 30 largest German companies in terms of book volume and market capitalization trading on the Frankfurt Stock Exchange. From the chart below, you can see the huge swings in the DAX price. In 2000 and 2007, deep bear markets hit hard.

Germany has a powerful economy and the model's performance has been exceptional. Manufacturing based economies run in long robust cycles. The best performing market timing cycle is a 3/2 Step Method and a 12 month MA. The 3/2 beat buy and hold by 2.1 times with 100% of the trades successful.

DAX: 1992 to 2010				
MA Cycle	8	10	12	14
B&H	41,198	39,249	43,494	43,494
Model	95,802	85,382	91,422	95,916
%Better	2.33	2.18	2.10	2.21
Trades	8	7	6	6
%Success	0.75	0.86	1.00	0.83
Med Gain	47.18	32.73	27.31	27.31
Med Loss	-10.28	-14.52	0.00	-5.34
Risk	0.64	0.64	0.66	0.67

DAX 3/2 STEP TIMING METHOD

Buy Rule: If the month end price is greater than the 12 month MA for <u>three</u> consecutive months, then buy.

Sell Rule: If the month end price is less than the 12 month MA for <u>two</u> consecutive months, then sell.

Action	Date	Price	Model	B&H
BUY	Apr-93	1627.2	10,000	
SELL	Oct-94	2071.6	12,731	12,731
In Cash			382	
BUY	Jul-95	2218.7	13,113	
SELL	Oct-98	4671.1	27,607	28,706
In Cash			920	
BUY	Aug-99	5270.8	28,528	
SELL	Dec-00	6433.6	34,821	39,537
In Cash			3,714	
BUY	Aug-03	3484.6	38,536	
SELL	Sep-04	3892.9	43,051	23,923
In Cash			431	
BUY	Dec-04	4256.1	43,482	
SELL	Feb-08	6748.1	68,941	41,470
In Cash			4,366	
BUY	Sep-09	5675.2	73,308	
SELL	Jan-11	7077.5	91,422	43,494

JAPAN NIKKEI INDEX

The Nikkei 225, more commonly called the Nikkei, is a stock market index for the Tokyo Stock Exchange (TSE). It has been calculated daily by the Nihon Keizai Shimbun (Nikkei) newspaper since 1950. It is a price-weighted average and the components are reviewed once a year.

The Nikkei is lower today than twenty-five years ago. Buy and hold in Japan has been a financial catastrophe. Market timing can help even in a market like this. Japan has a powerful manufacturing sector but it's weak on the consumer side. The people are prodigious savers. So, it's not what I consider a balanced index and it shows.

A 4/3 Step Model with a 12 month MA beats buy and hold by 5 times. A $10,000 investment in 1985 fell to about $8,000 with buy and hold. The model boosted it to $42,000. The model is only in the market 50% of the time. There were 7 trades in 25 years with a low 57% success rate. The median losing trade was under 5%.

Market timing can't work miracles but it came close in Japan. Considering the low interest rates in Japan for the last couple decades and terrible stock market performance, the timing model made a valiant effort. (The 3/2 Step Method also works in Japan).

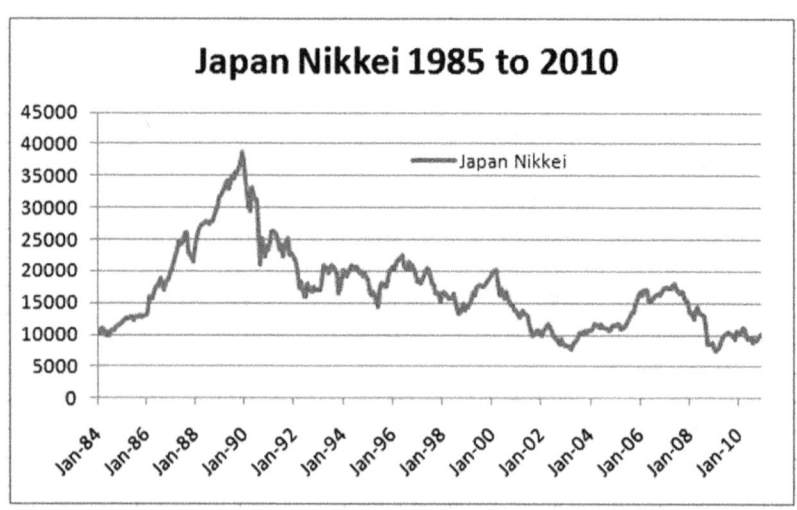

Japan: 1985 to 2010				
MA Cycle	8	10	12	14
B&H	8,131	8,004	8,348	8,061
Model	17,807	32,074	42,872	31,304
%Better	2.19	4.01	5.14	3.88
Trades	12	8	7	7
%Success	0.42	0.63	0.57	0.43
Med Gain	7.91	7.91	43.44	43.44
Med Loss	-7.91	-2.62	-4.80	-4.96
Risk	0.48	0.49	0.51	0.50

NIKKEI 4/3 STEP TIMINGMETHOD

Buy Rule: If the month end price is greater than the 12 month MA for <u>four</u> consecutive months, then buy.

Sell Rule: If the month end price is less than the 12 month MA for <u>three</u> consecutive months, then sell.

Action	Date	Price	Model	B&H
BUY	Mar-85	12590.0	10,000	
SELL	Apr-90	29585.0	23,499	23,498
In Cash			1,488	
BUY	Jun-93	19590.0	24,987	
SELL	Jan-95	18650.0	23,788	14,813
In Cash			396	
BUY	Nov-95	18744.0	24,185	
SELL	Dec-96	19361.0	24,981	15,378
In Cash			1,249	
BUY	Jun-99	17529.7	26,230	
SELL	Jun-00	17411.1	26,052	13,829
In Cash			1,693	
BUY	Sep-03	10219.1	27,745	
SELL	Nov-04	10899.3	29,592	8,657
In Cash			197	
BUY	Mar-05	11669.0	29,790	
SELL	Oct-07	16737.6	42,729	13,294
In Cash			1,638	
BUY	Sep-09	10133.2	44,367	
SELL	Jul-10	9537.3	41,758	7,575

139

Brazil IBOVESPA Index

As of December 31, 2010 the index had a market capitalization of US $1.54 Trillion, making it one of the largest in the world. On May 8, 2008, the São Paulo Stock Exchange (Bovespa) and the Brazilian Mercantile and Futures Exchange (BM&F) merged.

We have only 15 years of data for the Brazil market. Market timing works quite well with this rapidly growing index in what's called an emerging market. For Brazil, a 12 month MA with a 3/2 Step Model works best. We're able to beat buy and hold while receiving 4% interest when not invested. There were only 4 round-trip trades in 15 years and 100% of the trades were successful.

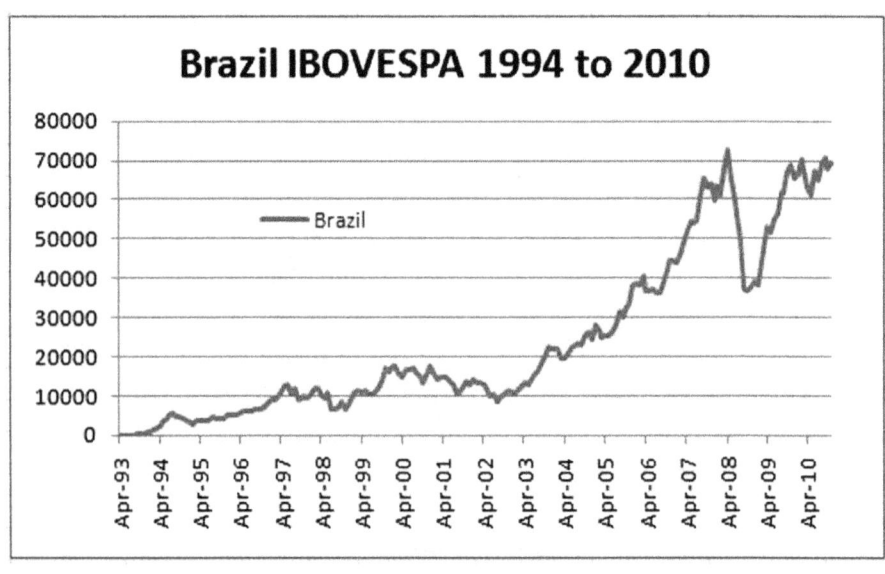

Brazil: 1994 to 2010				
MA Cycle	10	12	14	16
B&H	161,261	161,261	161,261	152,046
Model	108,107	181,665	136,961	163,829
%Better	0.67	1.13	0.85	1.08
Trades	7	4	5	4
%Success	0.71	1.00	0.80	1.00
Med Gain	30.98	127.57	127.57	121.03
Med Loss	-1.67	0.00	-17.12	0.00
Risk	0.66	0.68	0.69	0.71

IBOVESPA 3/2 STEP TIMING METHOD

Buy Rule: If the month end price is greater than the 12 month MA for three consecutive months, then buy.

Sell Rule: If the month end price is less than the 12 month MA for two consecutive months, then sell.

Action	Date	Price	Model	B&H
BUY	Oct-95	4128.4	10,000	
SELL	Nov-97	9395.0	22,757	22,757
In Cash			1,290	
BUY	Apr-99	11351.0	24,047	
SELL	Oct-00	14867.0	31,495	36,011
In Cash			3,254	
BUY	May-03	13422.0	34,750	
SELL	Aug-08	55680.0	144,155	134,870
In Cash			5,286	
BUY	Jul-09	54766.0	149,441	
SELL	Jan-11	66575.0	181,665	161,261

INDIA BSE SENSEX INDEX

The Bombay Stock Exchange SENSEX also referred to as BSE 30 is a weighted index of 30 well-established and financially sound companies listed on Bombay Stock Exchange. The companies are some of the largest and most actively traded stocks and representative of various industrial sectors of the Indian economy.

Data was first published for this index in 1998. A 12 month MA with the 4/3 Step Method works best for India. The returns of the timing method soundly beat buy and hold by 53% which includes 4% interest income for the out months. There were only three trades since 1998 and 100% were successful.

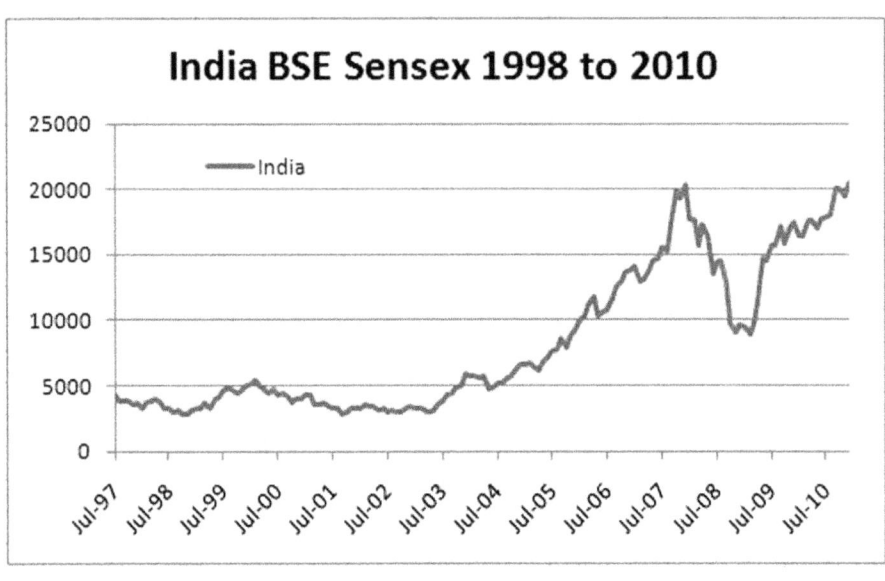

India: 1998 to 2010				
MA Cycle	8	10	12	14
B&H	55,277	49,005	46,211	40,348
Model	67,489	60,493	70,707	52,697
%Better	1.22	1.23	1.53	1.31
Trades	5	5	3	3
%Success	0.80	0.80	1.00	0.67
Med Gain	57.46	57.46	19.73	337.19
Med Loss	-16.13	-10.39	0.00	-9.95
Risk	0.67	0.68	0.68	0.70

BSE SENSEX 4/3 STEP TIMING METHOD

Buy Rule: If the month end price is greater than the 12 month MA for <u>four</u> consecutive months, then buy.

Sell Rule: If the month end price is less than the 12 month MA for <u>three</u> consecutive months, then sell.

Action	Date	Price	Model	B&H
BUY	Jan-99	3315.6	10,000	
SELL	Jun-00	4748.8	14,323	14,322
In Cash			1,528	
BUY	Feb-03	3283.7	15,850	
SELL	Jul-08	14355.8	69,296	43,297
In Cash			3,003	
BUY	Aug-09	15666.6	72,299	
SELL	Jan-11	18327.8	84,579	55,277

OTHER MARKETS

Moving average timing systems don't work well with many smaller stock markets. I consider markets marginal for timing if the price volatility between the buy and sell points becomes too large. This usually occurs as the timing cycle becomes longer. For example, Switzerland's SMI index can be timed with a 4/3 Step Model and a 16 month MA. With 4% interest for the out months, the model beats buy and hold by 70% with only 5 trades since 1991. 80% of the trades are successful and the one losing trade was -3.5%. The price swings, however, are quite large. It's a judgment call and I decided not to include markets with cycles longer than 14 months in this book.

18

TIMING THE NASDAQ

TIMING THE NASDAQ

The Nasdaq is the largest electronic screen-based equity securities trading market in the United States and second-largest by market capitalization in the world. As of January 2011, there are 2,872 listings. This exchange is a potpourri of huge companies and small firms. It's the go-to market for high tech and innovation.

Companies on the Nasdaq are a different breed than the staid giants of the S&P500. As such, it is more volatile and our market timing technique is different. We need more confirmation on price moves with the Nasdaq to indicate a change of direction. This concept was also discussed with gold and foreign markets. With the Nasdaq index, we use a moving average step system. We want to see four months of a rising moving average before we buy. We want three months of a falling moving average before we sell. Waiting to get the desired trend is worth your time.

Our Nasdaq timing system from 1973 to 2010 comes close to buy and hold on the Nasdaq. We get a high trade success rate of 90%. The median loss is in the 5% range. There's only 10 trades in forty years. The 14 month MA is the best in my judgment. The test results show symmetry as we change the moving average durations.

NASDAQ: 1973 to 2010				
MA Cycle	10	12	14	16
B&H	343,784	324,919	310,282	324,567
Model	235,386	271,396	293,084	222,818
%Better	0.68	0.84	0.94	0.69
Trades	14	11	10	8
%Success	0.86	0.82	0.90	0.88
Med Gain	19.87	27.22	17.78	32.03
Med Loss	-5.64	-5.64	-5.64	-15.29
Risk	0.69	0.71	0.71	0.76

In the early days, the Nasdaq was called the Over The Counter Market or OTC. It has matured and become the home for some prominent corporations like Apple and Microsoft. Market timing netted 94% of the index since 1973 but beat it by 15% since 1985. The timing system results have improved reflecting the increased maturity of the index.

NASDAQ: 1985 to 2010				
MA Cycle	10	12	14	16
B&H	96,225	92,850	89,614	96,328
Model	92,302	93,454	103,243	94,689
%Better	0.96	1.01	1.15	0.98
Trades	10	9	8	6
%Success	0.80	0.78	0.88	0.83
Med Gain	16.17	23.66	14.18	32.03
Med Loss	-5.64	-5.64	-5.64	-15.29
Risk	0.70	0.69	0.69	0.75

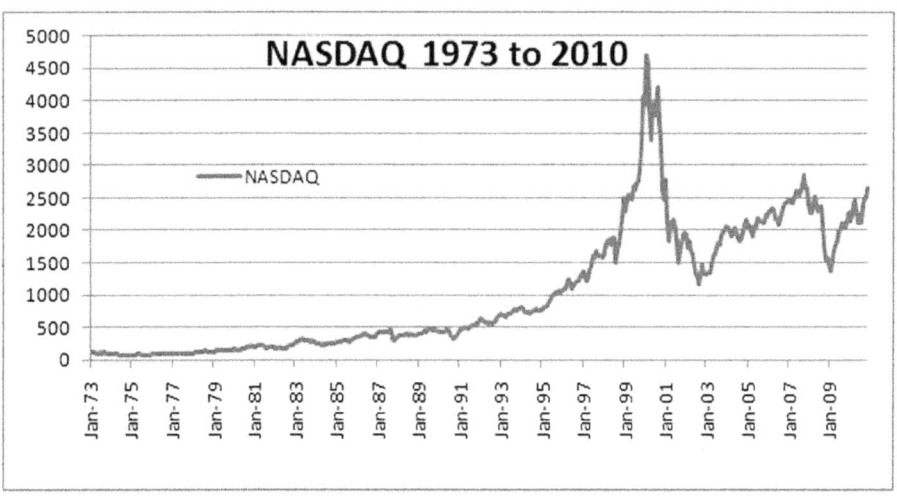

NASDAQ 4/3 STEP TIMING METHOD

Buy Rule: If the month end price is greater than the 14 month MA for <u>four</u> consecutive months, then buy.

Sell Rule: If the month end price is less than the 14 month MA for <u>three</u> consecutive months, then sell.

Action	Date	Price	Model	B&H
BUY	Jun-75	87.0	10,000	
SELL	Oct-81	195.2	22,436	22,436
In Cash			1,047	
BUY	Dec-82	232.4	23,483	
SELL	Mar-84	250.8	25,339	28,818
In Cash			1,098	
BUY	Apr-85	280.6	26,437	
SELL	Dec-87	330.5	31,139	37,979
In Cash			1,246	
BUY	Dec-88	381.4	32,384	
SELL	Mar-90	435.5	36,978	50,045
In Cash			1,602	
BUY	Apr-91	484.7	38,580	
SELL	Jun-94	706.0	56,190	81,126
In Cash			2,060	
BUY	May-95	864.6	58,250	
SELL	Nov-00	2597.9	175,032	298,544
In Cash			18,670	
BUY	Jul-03	1735.0	193,702	
SELL	Sep-04	1896.8	211,768	217,977
In Cash			2,824	
BUY	Jan-05	2062.4	214,592	
SELL	Jul-06	2091.5	217,615	240,343
In Cash			3,627	
BUY	Dec-06	2415.3	221,242	
SELL	Mar-08	2279.1	208,767	261,905
In Cash			13,222	
BUY	Oct-09	2045.1	221,989	
SELL	Jan-11	2700.1	293,084	310,282

19

TIMING THE COMMODITY INDEX

Commodities are the raw materials of the industrialized world. The list is dominated by petroleum products and also includes fibers, metals, rubber, grains and more. There isn't any one commodity index. There are a variety of mutual funds and ETF products that attempt to index this broad market and they do a good job.

Commodities are priced in the Futures Market. Futures are a marketplace dominated by industrial firms where they offer to buy and sell commodities in future months. For example, a farmer can effectively lock in a price on his soybean crop by selling a soybean contract for delivery some months out. A food processor may buy that contract to lock in raw materials costs. Speculators flit in and out buying and selling contracts hoping to profit on price changes caused by weather and other events.

Commodity prices are dependent on the business cycle and the world demand for raw materials. Thus, declining business activity can have sudden effects on various key commodities. Commodity prices are not closely correlated with stock prices or bonds and, for that reason, many investors like to include this asset class in a portfolio.

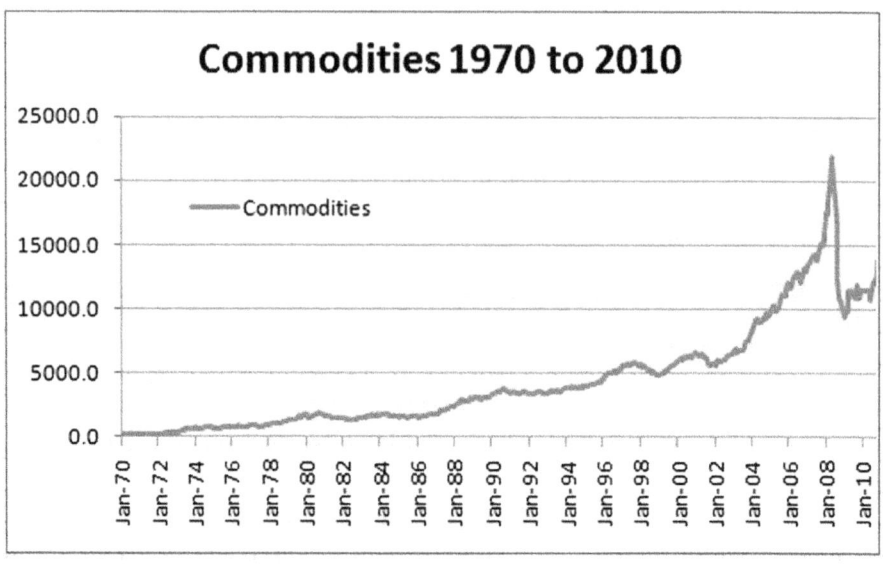

It is possible to market time this index with a high level of success. The best system is a 14 month MA with the 4/3 Step Method. Other timing durations are also quite good. The 4/3 model with reinvested interest at 4% during the out months beats buy and hold by 24% with only 9 trades over forty years. 100% of the trades were successful.

Commodities: 1970 to 2010				
MA Cycle	10	12	14	16
B&H	573,686	569,711	586,923	563,548
Model	548,863	678,290	728,504	640,009
%Better	0.96	1.19	1.24	1.14
Trades	10	9	9	9
%Success	0.90	1.00	1.00	1.00
Med Gain	54.50	54.50	56.19	56.19
Med Loss	-12.39	0.00	0.00	0.00
Risk	0.74	0.74	0.75	0.74

My price data was compiled from the paper Facts and Fantasies About Commodity Futures (http://www.nber.org/papers/w10595) by Gary Gorton and K. Geert Rouwenhorst. Data after 2006 was appended using prices from the DBC index. The timing results from 1990-2010 are similar to 1970-1990 thus showing excellent symmetry and consistency.

Investors should note my frequent admonition about moving average timing systems. The commodity index peaked in June of 2008. Look at the parabolic price spike on the chart. The 2002 trade made 50% but the results don't show that the timing model effectively didn't escape the 2008 crash. The model sold in November 2008 at half the peak price. This shows how price momentum models can't evade crashes of bubbles if the markets fall quickly. Moving average systems always buy after the trough and sell after the peak.

COMMODITY 4/3 STEP TIMING METHOD

Buy Rule: If the month end price is greater than the 14 month MA for <u>four</u> consecutive months, then buy.

Sell Rule: If the month end price is less than the 14 month MA for <u>three</u> consecutive months, then sell.

Action	Date	Price	Model	B&H
BUY	Mar-71	236.2	10,000	
SELL	Mar-75	702.8	29,748	29,748
In Cash			694	
BUY	Oct-75	746.1	30,442	
SELL	Sep-77	844.9	34,473	35,764
In Cash			575	
BUY	Feb-78	967.5	35,048	
SELL	Feb-81	1644.7	59,578	69,620
In Cash			4,766	
BUY	Feb-83	1481.4	64,344	
SELL	Sep-84	1624.6	70,566	68,769
In Cash			5,175	
BUY	Jul-86	1612.9	75,741	
SELL	Mar-91	3519.3	165,269	148,972
In Cash			9,365	
BUY	Aug-92	3554.6	174,635	
SELL	Apr-98	5551.8	272,754	235,005
In Cash			15,456	
BUY	Sep-99	5642.2	288,210	
SELL	Aug-01	6204.6	316,938	262,638
In Cash			13,734	
BUY	Sep-02	6283.9	330,672	
SELL	Nov-08	10880.2	572,543	460,556
In Cash			26,719	
BUY	Jan-10	11405.6	599,261	
SELL	Dec-10	13770.8	723,526	582,912

20
MANAGING YOUR ASSETS

Let's step through the investment process from start to finish with an example.

Susan is a forty-year-old successful artist and exhibits her work throughout the Western United States. She's too busy to spend time studying the financial markets and wants a portfolio that will grow and protect her money. She's had difficult time managing money by herself in the past. She hired a financial advisor based on a friend's recommendation. The portfolio he placed her in lost 25% of her money during the 2001 stock market crash. She switched advisors. In 2008 her portfolio dropped 40%. At this rate she'll never be able to retire or have any mental peace. Her new advisor moved some of her money into bonds when she voiced her worries. She can't afford to lose what she has left but knows these financial advisors can't protect her.

For 15 years she worked for Pharma Labs as a legal secretary, but quit at age 35 to pursue her art career. She accumulated vested pension rights at Pharma, but can't start taking the pension until she is age 60. She also contributed to a 401k program with Pharma and has $30,000 in her account. The 401k money is managed for Pharma Labs by the Boston Group Mutual Company. She also has $100,000 from an inheritance in a taxable account managed by the investment advisor. Spreading out her statements on the kitchen table, she looks over her financial accounts and lists her concerns.

The pension at Pharma Labs has 20 years until she can collect. She contacted the benefits officer at Pharma and learned the pension will be based on her average salary of $40,000 for the last 3 years she worked. It won't be adjusted for inflation. That means, for every year that goes by, the value of her future pension goes down due to inflation. (This is common). The cash-out value of the pension fund is now $25,000 and won't change. At age 60 she could collect $10,000 a year, but in inflation adjusted dollars it will be worth an estimated 60% less (3% x 20 years = 60% loss due to inflation). The $10k will really be worth only $4,000 a year at age 60 and the pension won't be adjusted for inflation – ever.

Her investment advisor has her $100,000 invested 70% in stocks and 30% in laddered bonds. He has the stock percentage spread across 4 stock funds. He charges her a 1% fee every year on the balance. She looked up the mutual funds on the Internet and found they have a front-end load fee of 5% and a 1.25% expense ratio each year. After reading *How to Invest If You Can't Afford to Lose*, she knows this is a very bad deal and could kick herself for never checking on these fees. She looks up the returns of the S&P500 for the last 5 years on the Internet by looking at the symbol VFINX. Her stock mutual funds have consistently underperformed VFINX over five and ten years. Now she's mad and feels like kicking someone else.

Susan checks on her $30k 401k account at Boston Group Mutual and finds out the firm is actually an insurance company. She thought the "mutual" in the name meant mutual fund. It turns out she's in mutual funds all right, but as a deferred annuity. Her yearly returns aren't very good and the fund fees are 1.3% plus other management fees. It's confusing.

The total value of her investments is $155,000.

Sitting back in the chair, she shakes her head and says out loud, "I need financial help". Susan gets on the phone and calls the Certified Public Accountant who does her taxes. She asks what he'd charge to help her move her money into a new portfolio and to give her some independent advice. She faxes him the statements and the page from her book that shows the Balanced #1 portfolio. He looks it over and calls back.

Two weeks later she visits her CPA. She's nervous and hopes what she has read and what he advises aren't in conflict. She's worried about doing the right thing. "Something has to be done or I'll never have financial security", she tells the CPA. He doesn't look up but just nods and continues filling out some forms. Glancing at his bookshelf, stacked with volumes on tax and accounting, her eye catches something familiar. It's a copy of *How to Invest If You Can't Afford to Lose.* Her entire body immediately relaxes as her friend, Fear, steps back. "*I'm safe!*"

The CPA hands her the completed IRA Rollover and other forms her employer needs to transfer the $25k pension fund money to Vanguard. He agrees that, with 20 years until age 60, she'll lose too much to inflation letting that money languish. Normally he would advise against exiting a pension, but he knows Susan has a good plan. "I'm happy to see you intend to roll over the pension money. Many people cash out of pensions and buy cars and vacations with the cash. That is always a bad thing to do. The taxes and penalties are enormous."

He next shows her the completed 1035 Exchange form and explains how this form is used to transfer annuity assets to another firm. This will save her $30,000 annuity from continued high fees. He says, "You'll earn at least an extra 2% each year by transferring your deferred annuity to Vanguard. They have the lowest fees in the business and work for the client, not for Wall Street"

"Here are the new account forms that show the various index funds your taxable investments will go into at Vanguard. I've called your financial advisor and he'll be sending you a check to close out your taxable account with him."

"I've also completed the IRS forms for a Roth IRA contribution. You have a good income and your business is doing well. It's essential to reduce your tax liability and save for retirement. You need to maximize your IRA contribution every year. In the future it also might be a good idea to set up a business pension plan."

"By the way, I really like your investment plan. I invest my savings much the same way." He glances at his bookshelf, smiles and says, "I'm 55 and can't afford to lose either." The CPA shows Susan a form with how the money will be invested.

Susan's Investment Plan

$155,000	Total investment assets
-25,000	1035 Exchange to the Vanguard Annuity
$130,000	Balance to Invest

Fund Symbol	% x $130,000	Amount
International	15%	19,500
S&P500	15%	19,500
Small Cap Value	15%	19,500
Aggregate Bond	30%	39,000
Short Term Bond	15%	19,500
REIT	10%	13,000
Total Invested		$130,000

"Your selected portfolio is a smart way to balance your assets for safety and good returns."

Susan asks, "How much should I save every year?"

Her accountant replies, "Save as much as you can and try to do it in a tax deferred account. It's impossible to predict what will happen in the future or what rate of return you'll receive. Online financial calculators and historical returns are useful, but only suggest what might happen. I'm optimistic you'll do well. I'd also suggest you gradually add some gold coins to your holdings and set them aside as a Core Holding that you never sell. In any country, life can take unpredictable turns and owning gold can turn the tide in your favor while others drown."

He continues, "One more thing, Susan. To maintain this effective plan, it's critical to re-balance your assets yearly. Let's make an appointment now to meet again in one year."

Susan's financial situation is typical of mid career people who need to energize their assets and stop the expense drain. She was lucky. She has an accountant who understands the power of indexing and the need for balance.

REBALANCE EACH YEAR

Portfolio money must be properly reallocated to maintain the original portfolio plan. Letting the assets grow haphazardly and without attention is like allowing a beautiful garden to be over-run by the fastest growing plants. Soon, it looks disheveled.

Once a year, readjust your portfolio so the starting percentages of each asset class are exactly the same as the year before. If the S&P500 (VFINX) rises more than the other assets over the course of a year, then you must reduce your holdings and shift the cash to the other assets that haven't done as well. Start each year with the right percentages.

It's tempting to let an asset be over-weighted, if it's doing very well. This is a mistake. Remember, you're trying to manage your money like a skilled pension fund manager would. They rebalance to manage risk and so must you. The beauty of my portfolios is they require only a once a year rebalancing. The rest of the year, you just ignore the market, if you wish.

If an asset class drops severely, don't panic. Stay invested. Shift more money into the losing asset next year, when the time comes to rebalance. Don't succumb to fear and assume it will keep falling. You can't outsmart millions of other investors. If the REIT market crashes what do you think will happen? Money will panic out of the REIT index and move into other assets. It just so happens that you own other asset classes so some other part of your portfolio will benefit. It may take a while for these asset shifts to work through the system, but it will happen.

Don't allow the week-to-week changes in your assets to become an issue. It's a normal process for things to jump around. I suggest you keep a journal and once a week or once a month write down the total value of your portfolio. If a severe correction occurs in the S&P500, your portfolio won't fall nearly as much because it's properly balanced. This little exercise will build confidence in your plan and show proof it's succeeding.

Be on guard against the constant fear-inducing and weak-minded analysis you hear in the media. Some of these people on TV sound very convincing as they predict what will happen next month or over the next few years. They're usually wrong and it doesn't matter how many advanced degrees they hold. They can't predict anything with consistent accuracy, because the markets adjust by the minute to new information. Policy changes by governments, wars, technology breakthroughs and many more criteria make long-term forecasts an exercise in futility.

If you start listening to "experts" and buy actively managed mutual funds in place of index funds, expenses will rise and performance will lag over time. You'll also encounter manager bias and mistakes. When you buy a non-index product you don't know what you're getting and things can change dramatically if a manager changes. This increases risk and unbalances your portfolio.

How to Withdraw Money at Retirement

The withdrawal rate, sometimes called the drawdown rate, is the percent of money you can safely spend from your portfolio each year without running out of cash in the future. Pension funds consider drawdown a critical component of good capital management and so must you. This withdrawal percentage is based on a simple formula. The portfolio's withdrawal rate plus the inflation rate must be less than the portfolio's earnings rate. In math terms it looks like this:

$$\text{Withdrawal \%} + \text{Inflation \%} < \text{Return \%}.$$

If you earn 8.5% on your portfolio and inflation is running at 3% per year then you have 5.5% in real return for that year. Theoretically, you could withdraw the entire 5.5% and your capital would remain constant. This is rarely recommended unless the investor is elderly and there's no concern about them outliving their money. For most people, a yearly drawdown rate of 4% is recommended. This can be increased or decreased depending on actual returns. Discuss the withdrawal rate with your fee-paid financial advisor or a smart CPA. This topic is very important.

Pension funds must make difficult decisions about drawdown rates. They're under pressure to increase benefits for retirees to compensate them for inflation. The effect of increasing health insurance costs is a major factor for the pension fund and the retiree. Most pensions are fixed and never provide a cost of living increase (COLA) to help with increasing costs. (This is sometimes called a PBI or Permanent Benefit Increase). Many government plans do provide a COLA.

Pension funds monitor their asset base using a different model, which you might wish to consider. They average the fund's returns for the last five years and use that number as the earnings rate. It's conservative and prudent to use an average return.

Here's an example from the Arizona State Retirement System.

Actual Returns of the Pension Fund

2010	14.9%
2009	-18.1%
2008	- 7.6%
2007	17.8%
2006	9.8%
Average 5 Year Return =	3.3%
Average 3 Year Return =	-3.6%

You can use a five or a three-year average to make sure you don't take out too much. If one high or low year skews the average, then make a conservative adjustment. Previously, I discussed how an individual could do better than pension funds because of flexibility and the ability to use low cost index funds. (It's a lot easier to invest $300,000 than $22 billion). Below are the actual after expense returns for the same five-year period using my Balanced #1 portfolio. Keep in mind - it was only invested 45% in stocks.

Actual Returns of Balanced #1

2010	13.0%
2009	19.4%
2008	-17.8%
2007	2.5%
2006	15.2%
Average 5 Year Return =	6.5%
Average 3 Year Return =	4.9%

The three and five year returns have beat America's best pension funds but must be adjusted for inflation. Subtract off 3% inflation from the five year average of 6.5% and you have a real average return of 3.5%. An investor can safely drawdown about 4%, based on the historical performance. In this case, a withdrawal rate of 5% or 6% for the current year is too much. So, if the investor needs cash for a car or a trip, maybe it's best to hold off for a year. If returns in the next couple years are better then it's not foolish to splurge a bit. I advise not to withdraw too much. It's best to always error on the side of caution.

PRIVATE PENSION FUNDS

An important issue for investors to consider is the pathetic, under-funded state of many corporate and municipal pension funds. Companies have used unrealistic return assumptions in order to minimize the money they must contribute to support future retirees. This has resulted in major pension funds being deep under water.

The Pension Protection Act of 2006 gave plans seven years to straighten things out. Many companies have responded by effectively shutting down their plans to new employees and requiring new hires to use a 401k with a variable company matching percentage. I say variable because the firm can match any amount it wants, depending on its financial circumstances. This should be a warning shot that you can't depend on corporate America to be your partner in providing retirement benefits in the future. Save as much money as you can.

In the globalizing world, corporations are under pressure to cut costs. They want to eliminate pension funds, health benefits and the historical relationship of trust and mutual support that has long existed in this country between employer and worker. The US government is complicit in this scheme and it will become obvious in the years ahead as the politicians change the social safety net programs.

Combined with an imminent real reduction in future Medicare and Medicaid benefits at the federal level, the average person had better start saving hard or they'll never be able to retire. The saving solution requires that people reduce unnecessary consumption. But, it's not just saving; the investor must extract the full amount they're entitled to from the financial markets. This can't be done if you're paying a financial advisor 1% of your assets every year and paying the big expenses charged by major mutual funds, which are also under-performing the index funds.

As I've shown previously, over time, the rate of return is more important than the amount invested each year. I've proven that a small initial investment can grow enormously if you don't lose money to market crashes. You may wish to consider my market timing ideas as a way to supercharge your returns and reduce risk. We can't do anything about market returns, but we can invest in smart index fund portfolios with low expenses and watch for warning signs and opportunity. If you can find like minded people willing to discuss my ideas it will help to know you're not alone.

Most Investors Don't Mange Money Well

I'm not overstating the costs of managed mutual funds and the deleterious effect this has on small investors. I'm intentionally understating the overall problem because I want to be fair to the minority of funds and advisors that do a good job. John Bogle, the highly regarded former Chairman of Vanguard Group and author of many books on mutual fund investing, states the problem in stark terms. He writes that the average mutual fund underperforms the S&P500 index by 3% and tax inefficiency takes away another 1%.

He doesn't stop there. For the average investor, it's much worse. They invest in speculative ETF products and specialty mutual funds and this habit of chasing returns demolishes their chances for success. These terrible results happen because much of the mutual fund industry has become a giant marketing machine focused on accumulating assets and not on safer returns and low fees. Investors fall for the hype and refuse to accept the clear evidence that the index fund approach is superior. Instead, they look at one-year returns and chase performance. They consistently incur high expense fees and receive poor returns.

Using a commission advisor may reduce the jumping around from fund to fund, but investors still get nicked for the 1% fee and the high fund expenses. In this book I've shown you how to use winning combinations of index funds to grow your capital. If you choose to ignore everything I've written, at least go to the library and read one of Bogle's books on mutual funds. I think you'll then look at this book with a new set of eyes.

Changing the Portfolio Mix Over Time

Each index fund and ETF I've presented is based on long-term correlations. It's unlikely you'll ever need to change the recommended percentages in each asset class. The mix is weighted towards American stock assets. Over time, it's likely that the US share of the world's stock markets will decline, as China and other nations become larger players in finance. This will be a gradual process.

This proportion can be automated by substituting the Vanguards Total World Index fund (VTWSX, the ETF version is VT) for the international and S&P500 portions of your portfolio.

Small Cap Value stocks are a core component of my portfolios because they deliver consistent and great returns relative to big companies. The US economy is gigantic and dominates world finance. Eventually, an index may be created to comprise a World Small Cap Value but we're not there yet. I'm in favor of a broad international approach, but we have to invest where there's liquidity and a broad selection of stocks. In addition, we need markets where regulations ensure fair practices and standard accounting practices that are rigorously enforced. That rules out buying a Chinese Small Cap Index for a long time.

21

REAL ESTATE

A significant percentage of small investors believe real estate is the ticket to wealth. As with any financial market, there's a time to buy and a time to sell. Within the real estate market, there's a broad diversity of products like commercial, rental, residential, warehouses and various classes of land.

Real estate is a business and it requires a realistic assessment of valuations and knowing when to buy, hold, and sell. I have a finance degree, have owned income property, have worked as a real estate agent, have college-level training in real estate valuation, and did professional real estate appraisals. I don't consider myself a real estate expert. To achieve that status I'd have to be currently active in the real estate business in a local market and have gained the knowledge to understand the market cycles of the region. My specialty is market timing and financial risk management and in those areas I do know a thing or two.

Let me start out by saying that residential real estate is not a good investment overall. The average home has increased in value about 5.5% per year since 1980. There's a lot of variation in yearly returns. The up years get people's attention, but the averages aren't too impressive. On the other hand, buying a home is not really an investment decision. It is one of the most sensible and gratifying actions a person makes in life. A sensible home purchase provides a comfort you can't equate with money.

Real estate is a local market business with big differences between regions in appreciation. Money can be made anywhere, if you buy low enough. Professionals are active in more than one segment of the market.

Knowing when to sell is a big problem for the non-professional investor. Riding prices up is very nice, but all markets peak and then fall to a trough somewhat above the last one. In short, real estate is cyclical and the big money is made not on gradual appreciation, but on capital gains. The last point is critical.

Big profits in real estate come from making a capital gain. You make the most money selling property for more than what you paid. Holding property forever will provide a gradual increase in wealth, but it won't make you rich very fast.

Numerous books tout themes like cash flow, leverage, fix-up, no-money-down, rental income and flipping. I don't dispute the validity of these ideas, but each concept is effective only at the right time and place and with the right type of property. People buy these books and make the mistake of thinking the financial concepts are universals and can be applied in all sorts of markets. That is certainly not true.

To be really successful in the real estate business, it's critical to have a feeling for the position in the cycle of the local economy in your area. You must also understand that real estate is not a cash flow machine that generates increasing income with each year. Real estate is costly to hold because of constant maintenance costs and taxes. The pros understand the various segments of the market and the cyclical nature of the business. They make the greater share of their income by trading property and not by holding it forever.

As with any other market, speculation may work for a while, but eventually the law of averages takes hold. Leverage eventually turns against the speculators and they fail, often dramatically. The best real estate investors are careful business people with the experience to recognize valuation opportunities. They have the financial staying power to wait out a mistake. If you intend to buy real estate then you need a strategy.

The best way to make a capital gain in real estate is to buy property after a cyclical price decline. Buy property in the path of progress. That means buying in an area that's going through rebirth or on the expanding "good side of town". You have to detect the trend early and act aggressively. Areas in decline will experience weaker capital appreciation and old properties are expensive to maintain. In short, risk is everywhere but so is opportunity.

If you can't afford to lose, then proceed carefully in real estate investment and don't believe the hype in the numerous books promising certain riches. It's a difficult business.

22

THOUGHTS ON INVESTING

In 1933, Dashiell Hammett wrote the classic mystery novel, The Thin Man. It's a great book with lively dialogue. William Powell and Myrna Loy played the major roles on the silver screen. In one scene, Nick Charles, the detective hero, is engaged in a conversation with a policeman at his ritzy apartment in the Normandie Hotel. His beautiful wife, Nora, interrupts him with a phone call from Quinn, his cocktail drinking buddy and stockbroker.

Nora came in and said Harrison Quinn was on the telephone. He told me he had sold some bonds I was writing off losses on and gave me the prices.

"Have you seen Dorothy Wynant?", I asked.

"Not since I left her in your place, but I'm meeting her at the Palma for cocktails this afternoon. Come to think of it, she told me not to tell you. How about that gold, Nick? You're missing something if you don't get in on it. Those wild men from the west are going to give us some inflation as soon as Congress meets, that's certain, and even if they don't, everybody expects them to."

"All right", I said and gave him an order to buy some Dome Mines at 12 1/2.

The year 1933 was the depth of the Great Depression, although it wasn't called that at the time. The stock market had fallen even lower since 1929 and businesses continued to fail. This was likely the cause of Nick's bond losses. A panicked Congress meant rising inflation might lie ahead.

Was Hammett giving his readers some market timing advice in that little scene? If so, it was a great call. The Dow Jones average was at about 50 and within five years it would be 150. Dome Mines stock would soar with a major find at its Ontario site. The linkages between gold, bonds, and stocks were understood seventy-five years ago and still exist today. As in Nick Charles' era, there's no shortage of market tips, sure things, wild guesses and market timers.

I use market timing but I know it doesn't work well for most investors. The majority of timing strategies out there are scientifically invalid, fail miserably at critical times or require too much effort and trading. It's risky to bet your wealth on things you don't understand. The portfolios I've presented in this book are easy to understand and will reduce losses from market crashes. My market timing strategies will save you from most long and costly market declines. If you do decide to use market timing, then the biggest problem you're likely to experience is your own psychology. Don't try to guess the market. Follow the strategy mechanically. It will take courage to buy back after a 30% drop in the index but that's what you must do.

Investors who are uncomfortable with market timing should focus on balanced investing. They're better off without timing, because it will just be a confusing and costly distraction. Timing may take the focus off balanced investing. Market timing is not necessary for the success of the portfolios I've presented. They have balanced stock assets and use safer bonds.

My timing methods are an additional step you can take to improve your returns. You must be willing to check the market prices monthly. My timing methods can still be valuable to the buy and hold investor because they can use this knowledge to shift portfolio allocations. For example, if my model warns to sell stocks, an investor may choose to delay an additional investment or reduce stock market exposure. It doesn't have to be all or nothing.

I developed advanced timing methods over the years because I had time on my hands, tremendous curiosity about the markets and have a lot of skill in computer programming. I don't explain all these methods because they'd soon be adopted by Wall Street or would be distorted and "improved" by opportunists selling subscription timing services. I have a web site (www.gleasonreport.com)

where you can follow my timing techniques but you're essentially placing your trust in my black box systems. On the other hand, I do publish the very infrequent buy and sell signals of my models as they occur. This full disclosure without retractions concept holds me to immediate accountability. I don't charge money for this service or sell anything. It's a lot of work and I reserve the right to discontinue it at any time.

Timing can be an excellent way to protect money from market crashes, but most developers of market timing methods haven't used a scientific approach and their ideas don't hold up under scrutiny. I've confirmed it through computer research. A few systems appear to work, but cause too many trades and this has expense and tax consequences. The best systems rarely trade and provide very specific warnings about market crashes. You're risking your savings following unproven methods and there's no guarantee they'll work when you need it. For most people, market timing is not advised unless you how it works and have access to the historical track record. That's what I've given you in this book.

Much of the short-term movement in financial markets is a mix of useless noise and legitimate transactions, speculations, fear and hope. There are, however, long and broad cycles that correspond somewhat with general economic activity and valuations. It's a waste of time to use rigid metrics to define proper valuations because asset classes are constantly adjusting to each other. Money, like water, seeks an equilibrium point, correctly balanced for risk and return. All are in constant flux. For that reason, the investor must not act on short-term fluctuations because these little adjustments don't tell you much.

There are, during the course of market cycles, points of extreme over valuation, but rarely do these episodes cause a crash. Normally they gradually resolve as market participants move money to take advantage of opportunity. A crash requires an extreme valuation discrepancy, a state of mass psychological delusion and finally a catalyst to set it in motion.

There's much at stake in financial markets. It is no wonder a lot of smart people have computers working hard looking for information they can exploit to profit from a trade. It's a tough business and a smart guy at home with his laptop will have difficulty beating the big money at the game. Some Wall Street firms make big bets on market trends and have access to trading information they can exploit. For example, if they know of big blocks of transactions hitting the market they can ride along with the trades and profit. This should be illegal but apparently it isn't because the big firms make tremendous profits trading for their own accounts.

The financial markets are a wild arena. Some investors like to think there must be a means to capture the trends and cycles with a key of some kind. That which is unknown, is mysterious. Some think the key to the problem might be found in the paranormal. This leads people to research various methods in an unscientific manner, since they've exhausted their limited training and abilities. They search for the answer in sequences of numbers (Fibonacci), geometric patterns (charting), sine waves, astrology, Kondratieff long-waves, and so forth.

I read a study a few years ago that about 40% of money managers actually believed there was validity to using Fibonacci numbers to make financial timing decisions. Fibonacci numbers are a simple sequence of numbers where each is a sum of the preceding two numbers (0, 1, 1, 2, 3, 5, 8, 13, 21, 34, etc). The sequence is useful in mathematics. It is observable in nature in ways such as how trees branch or in the curve of ocean waves, for instance.

A popular market timing method, using these numbers, is called Elliott Wave Theory. It's has no proof of application to financial markets, yet it's widely followed. In a nutshell, there is absolutely no market cycle value to this number set whatsoever. Mathematics is loaded with number sets and, though useful in math, they have no application to timing financial markets.

Another widely used method is Moving Averages (MA). These do work. A sensible MA system properly designed for an index can avoid the devastating losses of a crash. The MA is calculated by summing a daily or weekly range of occurrences representing a market index over time. Divide by the count of the observations and you get the average. That's simple. As a new observation is added, the oldest one drops off and the average is recalculated. This should show a past trend of the market and it does. It shows what the market did, but not what it will do in the future! A person using this technique will, by definition, always be buying late and selling a bit late.

I've performed computer tests on market data using moving averages. They can perform better than buy and hold but the cycle period has to be around one year. The waiting period above or below trend must be adapted to the specific market. Using short cycles of days and weeks will produce poor results. Many MA systems touted by people selling software and subscription services have frequent buy and sell signals because they use short cycles. This incurs high trading costs and frequent whipsaws.

Another popular technique you'll see all the time is called charting. People take an historical price data chart and then draw trend lines from the low and high points and project the lines into the future. Or, they give different price chart patterns names like "flag pattern" and "head and shoulders". Devotees love drawing these lines and writing articles suggesting what will happen next. It doesn't work but is wildly popular among technical analysts. I'll state it directly: Technical Analysis (TA) in the form commonly called charting is junk science! People who use this TA tool are doomed to failure. I have never seen a scientific test that proved charting works. TA is widespread on Wall Street and that should have Fear on high alert.

You cannot predict the financial markets with backward looking data. Moving averages look at the present price action and can detect a changing trend. Forward looking systems use statistically predictive indicators of future economic activity plus price divergences to present a probability of market direction. Future based systems are difficult to construct, are the most profitable and tend to morph over time.

I wouldn't want my money invested with a manager who uses charting, ultra short moving averages, Fibonacci Numbers, Elliott Wave, Dow Theory or the many bad ideas used to trick and abuse the small investor. Few managers will ever admit to using this stuff but many do.

Through investigation and experience, I've determined that long-term investing success won't be found in chart patterns and other hocus-pocus. There are indicators and data relationships that can suggest the probability an event may occur. However, once these indicators become known and put into widespread practice by other investors, their usefulness declines.

I have used market timing with good success since the late 90's. I exited the stock market before the 2001 crash and bought and sold during the down phase using my timing signals. I published a paper warning about the imminent 2008 crash. It takes a lot of confidence to bet against the trend and especially when the news and the experts disagree with you. Market timing has allowed me to grow my asset base and avoid steep losses. It has also allowed me to retire early and do what I enjoy.

A basic law of the universe is expansion and you'll also see it in culture, in nature and in the stock market. Market timing can avoid the occasional deep contraction phases that always follow expansion. If you exit the market prior to a severe downtrend then your assets will grow twice as fast. A simple asset allocation strategy will provide balanced profits on the expansion side.

At rare times nations go into a deep and destructive down cycle that may take decades to recover from. These periods usually follow war or when a nation falls into paranoia, deceit and arrogance. Assets are totally destroyed by depression, inflation and confiscation. Market timing can forewarn of these unfortunate periods and provide time to shift assets to gold. Gold is the ultimate asset and safeguards wealth during the financial night.

To summarize, a bad timing strategy will exit the market during the expansion phase or give a buy signal on the way down. This can be costly. A good system is simple, logical and has a high trade success rate. Even the best system is only an adjunct to other good investing practices.

CASH RESERVES

Every investor needs cash on hand to pay bills and for emergencies. This money is independent from my portfolios and can be held in a bank account or money market fund. You can also specify that dividends from your portfolio are either reinvested or deposited into a money market fund. All money market funds allow check writing.

WHAT IF THE POLITICIANS CAN'T FIX THE US ECONOMY?

I've discussed the uncertain future of the US economy. These concerns will become more prominent in the media over the next several years. Since we don't know what will happen in the years ahead, it's essential to hedge our bets. This means balancing a portfolio with offsetting asset classes. Placing all your money into one asset class is a speculation and almost always leads to investment failure.

I owned a bullion business in the 1970's and early 1980's. This was a period of rapid money printing and high inflation. We had interest rates over 12% as people fled the US dollar. Believe me, it was a scary time. In a future dollar panic we don't know how things will play out. This points out a few key concepts of investing.

- You can't predict the future based on the past.
- It's a serious mistake to allow Fear to control long-term planning.
- Good companies will survive regardless of what happens to the dollar.

WEAK DOLLAR AND INFLATION PORTFOLIO

If you are deeply concerned about the US dollar and inflation then I'd suggest an all-purpose, dollar-hedged portfolio. This is a good compromise portfolio that can adapt to inflation and recession. It preserves purchasing power during inflation. It consists of 25% S&P500, 25% foreign currencies, 25% gold and 25% US aggregate bond fund. It's acceptable to make small changes to the asset percentages. You can use high dividend, blue chip stocks or a world stock fund rather than the S&P500.

Another way to play a weak dollar is to buy the mutual fund PRPFX – The Permanent Portfolio. This excellent fund holds gold, stocks, bonds, and currencies. It performs well in inflationary markets and is adequate in normal years. The late Harry Browne pioneered this four asset class investing concept in the late 1970s and it is a good and balanced defensive strategy.

Accumulating Wealth

The portfolios and timing methods in this book are proven ways to grow your hard earned money. Wealth is built through work and sometimes luck. Investing grows wealth and protects it. You should use investing techniques proven successful over long periods of time.

After leaving the parent's home, young people have to fend for themselves. They form relationships and experience successes and failures that lead to a life path and a career. Thirty years of age may not be enough time to shake off the travails of a difficult early life, but by this time we can evaluate a person's energy level and good sense. Some habits of character and personality are better than others for gaining financial success.

People tend to congregate and attract others with like values and attitudes. Parents may bemoan their child's choice of associations, but it's not theirs to decide. Besides, once they leave home, lamentations have little effect on the outcome so it's best not to cast or accept blame.

Young people need to earn enough money before they can start saving. It takes time before most people have a decent job or business. The easiest way to make a good living is to do what comes easy. That is, have creative work that suits your temperament. Work becomes play. It's one of the best ways to propel a life into a groove of expansion. It brings financial success with the added benefit that boredom won't be a problem. Most people aren't so lucky and plod away at jobs they find just bearable. Many people can't move ahead because they can't see their path. Often a path is there, but is obscured waiting for a life change to jar the individual into a new direction. We hear stories of this happening all the time after a period of difficulty.

The best time to take chances is when young. To take advantage of a fortuitous circumstance, a person must be ready and prepared to act. Great ideas remain just ideas until a person puts thought into motion. I'll tell you this: Great opportunity knocks but once in the lives of most people. A person who is frequently intoxicated or lazy won't even get up to let opportunity in the door.

Money certainly isn't the most important thing. Still, money takes the sharp edge off of life and it is necessary for existing in the world. A person of modest earning power can still achieve a very comfortable retirement, if they make good relationship decisions and invest wisely as described in this book.

We've all known people seemingly born under a lucky star. Success seems to follow their every move. That's how it appears if you observe a person over the short time frame of a decade. But, poor decisions cause wrong actions that destroy finances, relationships and ruin careers. For all of us, life is always unraveling as it is being woven.

By the age of forty-five, I'd estimate that 80% of people have an attitude towards their jobs of dislike, boredom, lack of appreciation or no challenge. The lucky 20% are in careers that offer interesting experiences or satisfying financial rewards. Most of these outcomes are just plain luck and have little to do with intelligence, job training, or where you went to school. Things do or don't work out and it would take a seer to explain why.

You can never be sure if your attitudes and personality will resonate with others or if a chance meeting will offer an opportunity. Therefore, it's best to be adaptive and to act in a neutral way towards others all the time. Strong biases and opinions on anything from religion to politics can set people off (or on) and you may never know what you did to cause their response towards you.

Most people working for the government and large corporations will not be lucky in the career lottery. There's only so much room in the upper ranks. A series of decisions made by a succession of superiors gets a person stuck in a job and makes it hard to break out. Often the best career move is to leave, but that means abandoning seniority and job benefits. That's a problem when one has dependent children or other constraining family issues.

For the self-employed, the pressures of relentless competition, pressure upon profit margins and frequent changes in market conditions require a person to be always attentive and to take frequent risks. It can be a hard life and many would give it up for more security and regular hours. Still, I believe, the self employed are in a better position in the years ahead to prosper, since the wage growth of employees will be constrained by globalization. Business owners and independent contractors also have more control over their work environment and personal associations.

Some personalities can't adapt to the stifling culture and mundane routine of jobs in a bureaucracy. For example, a job as a community college administrator may offer security, but a creative person will usually find the leadership big on slogans and short on effective ideas. Creative people need freedom and expansion to be happy at their work.

When it's all said and done, we end up in occupations that offer varying degrees of financial reward, status, stress and opportunities for new experiences. I'm a big believer in seeking a healthy balance towards money and careers. Chasing the biggest salary isn't likely to bring great happiness, because no one will pay you large amounts of money unless you take on great responsibility and the stresses that come with it. For most people, a more rounded life with good personal relationships and a more modest income can be quite satisfying. I say that based on many years of observation and experience.

This brings us back to the objective of this book. We don't know how things will work out as we enter the world of work as a young and maturing person. People make decisions beyond our control and the die is often cast without our knowledge. Therefore, isn't it wise to begin a savings and investment plan at an early age? If things work out and we're one of the lucky ones, it's all icing on the cake. For the rest of us, years of steady financial accumulation can literally save your sanity in later life, when you can't take another five years in the job grind.

In later life, people have a good understanding of what they can do well. And, they have to be careful with their money because they can't afford to lose. After the age of 50, getting good jobs is difficult because firms don't see long-term potential in workers. At this point, some people make a decision to start a business. Often, this occurs after many years of work in a conventional career. If you go into business, make sure to keep retirement money safe. Don't put your (or your spouse's) future in jeopardy by being so sure of your ideas that you're blind to the possible pitfalls of a venture.

Be sure to setup a corporation or LLC and maintain a strict distinction between business and personal assets. Use tax deferred accounts to save. Retirement accounts are protected from creditors and lawsuits. Stiff tax penalties on early IRA account withdrawals are a strong incentive not to touch the money. Stay with a solid investment program, perhaps using the portfolios suggested in this book.

23

AN UNCERTAIN FUTURE

For the last 80 years, when people discussed the financial markets and stocks, they meant the US markets. American stocks accounted for over 50% of the world's actively traded issues. Most of the major brand names of products we purchased were owned by American companies and were sold around the world. This was the era of powerful industrial unions and well paid blue-collar workers. Congressmen didn't dare alienate the working class, because it usually meant they would be a casualty in the next election. Government, industry and labor formed a tight partnership and maintained a balance between disparate interests for the betterment of the country. There were tough periods for the economy, but when taxes, wages or profits became unbalanced, the voters set things right through the polls or labor strikes.

Over the last twenty-five years the situation has changed. In 1985 89% of Fortune 100 firms offered defined benefit pensions to workers. By 2002 it was down to 50% and by 2009 it was at 17%. At the same time, the wealth of corporate executives has soared. In 1960, the average CEO earned 50 times the average worker's salary. They earned 100 times in 1990 and, by 2009, it was over 400 times.

In 2010 the richest 1% of Americans owned 42% of the nation's financial wealth. The top 5% owns 69% of the wealth. These ratios, overall, have changed surprisingly little over the last 70 years. In 1922, the top 1% controlled 36%. The striking disparities between rich and poor are most pronounced in America, but in Europe the top 1% generally holds over 50% of the wealth. It's fair to conclude that concentration of wealth is a worldwide phenomenon. As Asia becomes richer, we're likely to see a similar situation.

As a vehicle for building wealth, financial assets are the key. Despite the ups and downs of the markets, owning shares in corporations is a proven way to grow wealth. That's why I urge every investor to own some stocks in their portfolio even if you are extremely risk averse. In the future, ownership of foreign stocks and having a global perspective will be increasingly important. Globalization is here to stay.

The Off-Shoring of Jobs

Today, most consumer goods are made somewhere other than America and Europe. Everyone's concerned about it. I'll bet you check the labels on products you buy to see where things are manufactured. Workers here will continue to endure the slow equalization in wage parity between East and West. And, what a difference there is. The average American likely earns about $20 per hour with benefits whereas in China it's about $1.00 per hour. This means the wage equalization process has a long time to run. But, it's more than wages. This balancing act also includes the regulatory environment, access to natural resources and geopolitical factors.

Simply put, the wage disparities between the West and East became so large and the ocean of low wage workers became so appealing that the trickle became a flood of firms moving operations to Asia. This happened because China effectively dropped Marxism as its national motto, embraced open markets and offered its unemployed masses to the world market. Other Asian nations followed and they now have the world's best economic growth rates.

Several years ago, the politicians told us we only needed to make a shift to jobs in the technology sector and work as computer programmers, microchip engineers and technical writers. Those jobs also are going offshore. Salaries for computer programmers in the US are stagnant. There are more English speakers in India than in America. The Chinese are now learning English in grade school.

Despite the negative impact in America, globalization is obviously a big positive for many people around the globe. They now write computer programs and solve technical problems for US based companies. As more people become employed, educational levels rise along with quality of life and longevity. Increased interaction between nations reduces the potential for misunderstanding and expands cultural understanding.

Jobs may go overseas but the headquarters of major companies have stayed in the United States. That's because of the protections provided by America's outstanding legal system and a culture of respect for private property. Asia is a long way from rising to that plateau.

Will the Dollar Collapse?

America borrows vast sums of money from China and other nations. China is willing to lend the money and accept depreciation of its dollar holdings if it can continue to gain market share from the West. . The United States wants a huge military and China wants to grow its economy. This arrangement is suicidal for America but there's little will to change. This is the Chinese way of winning without confrontation.

America must cut spending. Changes are required in entitlement programs and military spending. People assume it's impossible for politicians to make the tough decisions necessary to save the dollar and close the fiscal gap. If you've never worked in government, it's easy to mistake a *lack of action for a lack of attention*. Political leadership roles require a mastery of survival techniques and an ability to deflect accountability. That's because a politician is always under scrutiny and subject to attacks by opponents. The politicians will act when they know they'll personally survive the crisis.

Foreigners have been buying US bonds and helping to hold down interest rates in America. It's the calm before the storm. America's terrible balance of trade means those dollars will soon be allowed to purchase controlling ownership in US firms. It's just a matter of time before Americans no longer control many well-known companies. This has implications for America's ability to tax corporate profits if firms eventually do move outside the US.

The low US interest rate environment, made possible by Asian purchases of bonds, won't continue indefinitely. The Federal Reserve has used Quantitative Easing (money printing) as a means to buy treasury debt because foreign buyers have become cautious and with good reason. They see the problems ahead.

I believe America is in the early stage of reducing its military footprint around the globe. This contraction is being forced by untenable budget deficits. At the same time, oil prices will continue to rise. Access to oil may be impaired by political strife in oil producing nations. This means cuts in military spending will be resisted further exacerbating budget deficits. Major military cuts will come slowly. Congress will likely go after domestic entitlement spending first. This will threaten the savings and expectations of older workers. It seems certain that a long period of difficulty is ahead. The shift of growth to Asia is not positive for the dollar's future as the world reserve currency. Now, more than ever, investors need to adopt a global investment view.

Markets Confound the Analysts

There's never a shortage of commentators stridently offering reasons why the stock market is overpriced and destined to fall. Their reasons usually make sense looking in the rear view mirror and are almost always wrong. Financial markets are forward looking and discount information. If it's in the news it's been discounted. It's extremely difficult to make an accurate prediction for what will happen a couple years out.

The markets sometimes seem irrational and consistently defy logic. That's because the natural state of the world economies is expansion amid continual readjustment. To bet against the markets due to the concerns of some commentator is usually a bad idea.

Another key thing to understand is that markets drop much faster than they rise. A bull market may take six years to peak but only 18 months to decline. Projections of multi-year recessions, even if they come true, do not result in years of stock declines. The wash out happens much faster and travels to the extreme downside in a short period. This lack of synchronization between the economy and the stock market always seems to perplex people. It's just the market reacting to what's known and doing it quickly. Exaggerated declines are the result of investor panic. Panic is eventually followed by a rebound, with prices readjusting among the asset classes.

Despite the hand wringing by experts and commentators, we are witnesses to a truly revolutionary period in financial market history. Globalization requires corporations and nations to operate efficiently if they want to stay competitive. Stock markets are opening to a new group of investors as wealth increases in Asia and other emerging economies. This can stabilize mature economies and offer capital to young ones.

An Investment Plan of Action

It's improbable that anyone can predict how the huge changes ahead will impact the financial markets. We can't be certain our leaders will do the right thing. Economies and policies overseas are also very hard to forecast. Successful investors in every age have faced these types of uncertainties and that's why they diversified their assets. Sitting in cash is a speculative behavior and quite risky.

America will become much more of a saver nation out of necessity. It may be too late for baby boomers who haven't saved, but the next generation could do quite well if they invest rather than spend.

People with money properly invested in a conservative and broad mix of assets are taking a course of action shown to have worked in the past. The portfolios I've presented in this book have performed well over the years and likely will protect your money in the future. I urge you to diversify your assets. Rebalance your portfolio once a year. Focus on balance and not on speculations or obtaining the highest short-term returns.

24

SUMMATION

I've stressed repeatedly the need to respect Fear and to listen to him. He is the composite of all your inevitable failures and disappointments. Fear of the financial markets tends to freeze people into inaction. What's really needed is an understanding of ways to balance assets to prevent disastrous losses. Fear must listen to knowledge. The portfolios I've suggested are knowledge you can use today to lower your portfolio risk and improve your returns. For the more enterprising investor, I've presented my market timing ideas that are mathematically proven to beat buy and hold and with lower risk. They have protected assets from most of the crashes of the last ten years. No small accomplishment, I think you'll agree.

The globalization trend will continue and money will ebb and flow among markets always seeking the best opportunities for profit. Taking advantage of world markets is the smart way to invest. The timing methods I've presented in the book let you detect the trends. You can allocate your money with a reasonable degree of confidence that your trade will be successful. Any losses will likely be small.

Never invest in anything you don't understand and maintain a healthy skepticism toward the promises of the financial services industry. Commission advisors are unlikely to recommend index funds or this book. That's because it's hard to skim high fees if the customer is well informed. After reading this book, you should be able to recognize unbalanced portfolios, high-fee funds and self-serving advice. It's your money so don't be shy about asking tough questions of a financial advisor. Don't pay anyone a percentage of your assets and refuse to pay expensive mutual fund fees.

Success in any endeavor requires skillful action. Anyone who succeeds at investing has made his or her share of mistakes. With time and experience, we do fewer dumb things because we listen to Fear and gain knowledge. I can't guarantee your portfolio will make money every year. However, the historical research shows that diversification and market timing greatly reduce the chances of losing.

In the future, the core concepts of investing will remain the same. Steady saving and investing, with a well-balanced and low expense portfolio, will build wealth. A modest income certainly doesn't prevent financial success. The investor must always be careful not to chase performance and short-term results. It's useful to keep an open mind towards investments. Start off cautiously, educate yourself and listen to others with various ideas.

The ideas presented in this book have worked in the past and will provide balance and opportunity in the future. If they improve your life, then I've been successful. To the investor who can't afford to lose, I offer my best wishes for your success.

www.ingramcontent.com/pod-product-compliance
Lightning Source LLC
Chambersburg PA
CBHW071426170526
45165CB00001B/408